The Gospel
Unplugged

The Gospel Unplugged

Turning Up the Volume on Songs That Rock Your Soul

Rich Wagner

Revell
Grand Rapids, Michigan

Published by Fleming H. Revell
a division of Baker Publishing Group
P.O. Box 6287, Grand Rapids, MI 49516-6287

Printed in the United States of America

Library of Congress Cataloging-in-Publication Data
Wagner, Richard, 1966–
    The Gospel unplugged : turning up the volume on songs that rock your soul
/ Rich Wagner.
        p.   cm.
    Includes bibliographical references.
    ISBN 0-8007-3052-6 (pbk.)
    1. Contemporary Christian music—History and criticism. 2. Music—Biblical teaching. I. Title.
ML3187.5.W33 2005
782.25—dc22   2005005250

Published in association with Yates & Yates, LLP, Literary Agents, Orange, California.

www.gospelunplugged.com

Interior design by
Brian Brunsting

To Kimberly

Contents

Introduction

Music of all kinds can take hold of us. A song can influence the way we think, shape the way we live our lives, and actually become part of who we are. In an unexplainable way, music is able to penetrate deep inside of us—moving from the ear, mind, emotions, and spirit down to the soul. This influence is exactly why some Christians have always been leery of rock music: because music in the wrong hands can be such an effective weapon used by Satan to draw you away from God. But on the flip side, Christian artists can also use music's creative power to help you draw closer to Jesus Christ and strengthen your relationship with him.

Oxford don and Christian author C. S. Lewis once said that a sure sign of a nonreader is that he will use "I've read it already" as a good excuse against reading a book. Lewis adds, "Those who read great works, on the other hand, will read the same work ten, twenty, or thirty times during the course of their life."[1] I feel the same way about music. Like a great book or film, a great song should never be consumed like a fast-food burger—eaten on the run as you move on to the next thing. Instead, a great song is meant to be experienced, mined for all it's worth, listened to again and again, and discussed to the wee hours with others.

What makes a song worth all this attention? Three things, I think. I believe a great Christian song will teach us truth, express who we are, or reveal part of God's nature to us. Let me explain.

First, great Christian music teaches us. We can discover God's truth through the imagery, word pictures, and emotion contained in a song in ways we may not always be able to through a book or a sermon. Jars of Clay's "Worlds Apart," for example, gets to the heart of what true discipleship is in a way so piercing that you would have a hard time matching it even if you read a five-hundred-page theological tome. And by living out the truth packed inside Sixpence None the Richer's "We Have Forgotten," you can transform an otherwise meaningless existence into a life of eternal significance.

I recently experienced the teaching power of music as I went through a long period of searching for God's direction for my life. Sensing a nudge from God, I took a leap of faith and moved across the country, trusting that he would fill in all the unknowns along the way. But when answers were slow to come by, I began to stress out and question whether God was really going to help me. I read books about faith and studied the Bible, but I still struggled with completely trusting him. One day I listened to "Deep End" by the Newsboys as I drove down the highway. I had heard the song many times before, but this time the lyrics grabbed me by the collar and wouldn't let go:

To take this step of faith
Don't need to be scared

Turn worry into wonder
Dissolve the fear

As I listened to these lyrics over and over, God transformed me. All of the head knowledge that I had taken in up to that point instantly fell into place. I finally began to understand what it means to simply hand over my worries to Christ and then watch in wonder as he works in my situation. That's the kind of freedom and trust that Jesus talks about all through the Gospels. "Turning worry into wonder" became my motto for that whole period of my life. God used "Deep End" to teach me a truth that I was having trouble picking up from other sources.

Second, great Christian music helps us express ourselves to God in new ways. Most contemporary Christian songs you listen to on the radio or on CD are enjoyable for a time but then fade away as the next big hit comes along. However, once in a while a song comes along that rocks our world; it taps into something that is already inside of us, just bursting to come out. Not only do we identify with the song, but the song acts as something more powerful—it helps give us an identity. I first heard Steven Curtis Chapman's "For the Sake of the Call" around the time I was wrestling with the issue of what it means to "die to yourself" as a disciple. As I listened to the lyrics, I felt like Chapman had tapped into my head when he wrote the lines, "We will abandon it all / for the sake of the call." That was me, the exact commitment that I wanted to make to God! Through his song Steven Curtis Chapman gave me the perfect way to express to Jesus the decision I had made.

Third, great Christian music gives us a taste of the infinite. A song can also reach deep into our souls and awaken us to who God is. I think the rarest of songs can even give us a foretaste of God's glory. For example, whenever I hear *"Agnus Dei,"* performed originally by Michael W. Smith and now also by Third Day, my heart is immediately transported to another place. The beauty of this worship song offers me a sort of musical window into heaven, a glimpse of the glory that is to come.

The film *The Shawshank Redemption*, a story of hope winning out in the midst of a dark prison, speaks of this "otherworldly" quality of music. In one scene an opera song is played over the prison's loudspeaker. Reflecting on the impact that the music had on the inmates, one prisoner says:

> I have no idea to this day what those two Italian ladies were singing about. Truth is, I don't want to know. Some things are best left unsaid. I like to think they were singing about something so beautiful it can't be expressed in words and makes your heart ache because of it. I tell you, those voices soared, higher and farther than anybody in a gray place dares to dream. It was like some beautiful bird flapped into our drab little cage and made those walls dissolve away. And for the briefest of moments, every last man in Shawshank felt free.[2]

In the same way, great Christian music can make us feel alive and free and allow us to experience the presence of Jesus Christ in ways that are rare in our practical, commonsense world.

The Gospel Unplugged is divided into five parts, each covering different aspects of life. In part 1 we'll explore three songs, each of which reveals something about the amazing love that God has for us. In part 2 we'll discuss songs that point to the freedom and identity we can experience in Jesus Christ. Part 3 will find us diving into life's meaning for the Christian. In part 4 we'll look at songs that confront tough issues we face when living out our Christian faith. And in part 5 we'll explore songs focused on how to keep our eyes fixed on Jesus Christ in this complex, modern world.

As you read through *The Gospel Unplugged*, I encourage you to dive into the meaning behind each song's lyrics, discover their biblical foundation, and get practical about how you can apply these truths to your life. To help you out, I've included two things at the end of each chapter: an Action Steps box providing specific challenges to get you started living out the truth seen in the song, and a Diving Deeper box giving you Bible verses, books, and films that you can turn to for further exploration of the song's theme.

One last thing . . . music is an art, not a science. As a result, lyrics can be interpreted many ways. While I attempt to tap into the meaning these artists had in mind when they wrote the song, I may occasionally spring from their lyrics into directions the artist never intended. So as you read through this book, keep in mind that I am offering *an* interpretation of the lyrics but not necessarily *the* interpretation.

That's what's so great about music. Songs and the artists who write them allow us to live and experience the music for ourselves on our own terms. Because when we dive deeper into our favorite playlist, we elevate the songs from piped-in background music to our own personal soundtrack. And that's the real purpose of *The Gospel Unplugged*: to study songs that wave our hands, bob our heads, shake our fists, and rock our souls.

Rich Wagner
September 2004
Princeton, Massachusetts

Part One

God's
Boun

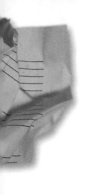

But while [the prodigal] was still a long way off, his father saw him and was filled with compassion for him; he ran to his son, threw his arms around him and kissed him.

Luke 15:20

Oh refuge of my hardened heart
Oh fast pursuing lover come
As angels dance around Your throne
My life by captured fare You own

Jars of Clay, "Hymn"

dless
Love

1

Clocking God

Nasty. Ugly. Hopeless. Words like these quickly come to mind when we spend a few minutes watching TV or reading the front page of the local newspaper. Sins that just a generation ago brought shame and humiliation are today not only accepted but actively promoted. The world's twisted values are obvious just by clicking the remote: as CNN chronicles a famine that is starving millions of African children, the E! channel devotes hours to the latest Hollywood drivel. And just by thinking about tragedies like the Southeast Asian tsunami, we come to realize that suffering is everywhere and always seems to pick on the most innocent of people.

As Christians we know in our hearts that above all this chaos, God is in control. But that may not stop us from butting heads with him over what he ought to be doing to fix this mess. Why does God allow suffering and endless sinning to continue? Why should believers be forced to experience such hardship?

In the midst of these questions, Chris Rice's song "Naive" deals with the differences that often exist between the way Christians look at the sad state of the world and the way God sees it. The only way we can ever bridge this gap and make sense of the situation, Rice shows, is by focusing on God's underlying motivation. Only then will we be able to grasp why God works the way he does.

Out of Touch

You and I live in a time that could perhaps best be called the Jaded Age. Through media, teachers, friends, and sometimes even parents, we are taught to look at life skeptically, even pessimistically; we are to assume the worst. But if you had grown up a hundred years ago, chances are you would have a much more optimistic view of the world. Back then, common sense said that people were "basically good" and all that was really needed to stomp out evil was better education, government, and technology. Many people, including Christians, fell into the trap of believing that the human race could create some kind of heaven on earth by sheer willpower.

But two world wars, concentration camps, nuclear weapons, and frequent environmental catastrophes drowned out this kind of naive thinking. As the Bible has pointed out all along, better schools and high-tech gadgets don't change the basic fact that people are sinful creatures. Or as Jeremiah puts it, "the heart is deceitful above all things, and desperately wicked" (Jer. 17:9 NKJV). Fast forward now to our Jaded Age, a time in which the dreams from generations past have been thrown out and replaced by pessimism. Evil looks like it is winning. God seems so far away, out of touch with reality.

As "Naive" begins, Chris Rice raises tough questions Christians commonly ask God about why he seems uninvolved:

How long until You defend Your name
And set the record right?
How far will you allow the human race
To run and hide?

We read bold statements by Paul like "God cannot be mocked" (Gal. 6:7) yet all around us hear God's name smeared at school or work. We thumb over to Psalms and come across the verse "The LORD is known by his justice" (Ps. 9:16) yet wonder why the bad guys always seem to finish first. When confronted with these apparent contradictions, we easily lose faith and react against God.

We could all grow cynical and simply give up on him. The reality of evil has always been used as a major argument against the existence of a loving God. Skeptics argue exactly what Chris

Rice wonders about in "Naive"—that "a God who's good would never let the evil run so long." They conclude that God can't be both all-loving and all-powerful; he either doesn't love everyone or is powerless to stop bad things from happening to them.

Alternatively, instead of becoming jaded and cynical, we can simply look at the state of the world and become disheartened. U2 captures this sense of weariness in their song "Peace on Earth." Lead vocalist Bono sings about wanting heaven on earth now, but his experiences with war and strife have left him demoralized and tired. He is worn out by the promise that there's going to be peace on earth and cries out to Jesus: "Can you take the time / to throw a drowning man a line?" Ultimately, since "hope and history don't rhyme," the song concludes that we will never experience peace while still on this earth.

Finally, while some people give up or grow weary, others have a completely opposite reaction: they try to take matters into their own hands. Frustrated by God's seeming inaction, they start to act like God's "terminator," seeking justice in the world at all costs. When we feel compelled to take on this role, we become willing to wrestle control away from God because, deep down, we conclude he isn't up to handling the situation. We question, as "Naive" puts it, whether we can really "leave the timing of this universe to bigger hands."

We question whether we can really "leave the timing of this universe to bigger hands."

Well-meaning Christians do this all the time. Instead of speaking out for God's holiness in a spirit of Christian love, they become judge, jury, and executioner for the sins of society. Speaking out against abortion or homosexual marriage, for example, some Christian protesters become so hateful of sin that they forget all

God's Boundless Love

about trying to love people trapped in the web of these sins. In the process they end up sounding like hatemongers to the very people Christ wants them to reach out to.

Questions

When we attempt to make sense of the world from a human standpoint, questions will always swirl up all around us. Chris Rice packs these sorts of questions into the chorus of "Naive":

> Am I naive to want a remedy
> For every bitter heart?
> Can I believe You hold an
> Exclamation point for every question mark?
> Yeah
> And can I leave the timing of this universe
> To bigger hands?
> And may I be so bold to ask
> You to please hurry?

These four questions raised by Rice in the chorus are revealing. When we look for their answers, we can discover four biblical truths that are essential to grasp if we want to have peace with how God works in the world.

First, we are born with a need for justice. God must have created people with some sort of "justice gene," because Christians and non-Christians alike instinctively feel this need. When we comfort a friend who struggles with a "bitter heart," we will always cry out for a "remedy" for her pain. So too, in the political world, conservatives and liberals disagree on the answers to society's problems, but they both claim justice as their goal. Since God gave us this longing, our hopes for justice are not naive. Such a desire is a good thing, so long as we do not get out in front of God in its pursuit.

Second, we are born with a need for answers. We not only have something inside of us that yearns for justice, but we also have a need for answers to the "why?" questions. We need to know that God holds, in the words of Rice, "an exclamation point for every question mark." When something bad happens, we will always find tragedy easier to accept if we can make sense of why it occurred.

At times, God will let us in on the answer. But not always. In fact, the reality is that we may never know the answers to our "why?" questions as long as we walk on the earth. Yet just because answers may be slow to come does not mean that we will never receive them. For the Christian, the question is not *if* we will get answers but *when*. Oswald Chambers spoke about God's amazing promise:

> There will come one day a personal and direct touch from God when every tear and perplexity, every oppression and distress, every suffering and pain, and wrong and injustice will have a complete and ample and overwhelming explanation.[1]

As a Christian, you can have full confidence that one day God is going to supply answers to the questions that haunt you in the here and now.

Third, we are called to let go of these needs today and let God be God. We may feel justified in demanding justice and answers here and now, but that is not an option that is open to disciples. Instead, we are called to "leave the timing of the universe to bigger hands." Turning the hands of your clock back to God's time can be one of the hardest tasks of a Christian. But when you finally throw out your list of demands, God will give you a peace in allowing him to be God instead of trying to do it yourself.

Fourth, the only way to live in a sea of questions is to take on an eternal perspective. Because God's timing is not ours, we are called to be patient. But as Rice points out in his final question of the chorus, we easily claim patience, then tack on a "please hurry" when talking with God. In fact, as if to stress the fundamental gap between God's timetable and our own, Rice ends the song on an impatient note:

> And may I be so bold to ask You, to ask You,
> To ask You
> How long?

Rice's impatience highlights the fact that if we think of our lives as being only eighty years on this earth, we will always demand justice and answers from God *now*; we'll always tack a "please hurry" onto our prayers. But if we begin to consider our lives in light of eternity, we can begin to get a glimpse as to how God sees things. Only when we have an eternal perspective can we have peace in a world of injustice and unanswered questions.

Someday every knee *will* bow and every tongue *will* confess that Jesus Christ is Lord (see Phil. 2:10–11). Someday there *will* be no more sorrow or tears (Rev. 7:17). And, yes, as Revelation 21:1–4 promises, we really *will* one day experience that elusive "peace on earth." The key for disciples, however, is realizing that God is going to make these realities happen according to *his* clock—not Rice's, or Bono's, or yours, or mine.

Enough

At the close of the first verse, Chris Rice longs for a day when Jesus Christ will say "that's quite enough." That brings to mind times in the Old Testament when God spoke those words and followed them up with swift and bold action. He drowned everyone on earth but Noah and his family. He wiped out the cities of Sodom and Gomorrah with fire. He struck dead an Israelite who tripped carrying the ark of the covenant. And he made sure disobedient Israelites were conquered by other nations. All of these judgments, however, were just warm-ups for what is to come. And that judgment is what Rice is asking for during the bridge of "Naive":

> But when will You step into our sky blue and say
> "That's quite enough, and your time is up"?

Jesus will "step into our sky blue" when he returns to the earth a second and final time. Depending on your relationship with Christ, you will hear either the most terrifying or most blessed words imaginable from Jesus: "That's quite enough, and your time is up." At his second coming, evil and suffering will be stomped out once and for all, and God's justice will be served.

For two thousand years, Christians have been urging God to say "that's quite enough"—and pronto! Indeed, hardly anything seems more natural to ask for when we feel lost in a sea of sin and suffering. But if God hates evil so much, why hasn't Christ returned yet? Why has he waited so long? Chris Rice lets us in on the secret in the second verse of "Naive":

> I say it's because You're good
> You're giving us more time
> 'Cause I believe that You love to show us mercy

The answers to all of the questions Rice has for God in "Naive" are rolled up into those words. As Rice reveals, **God's clock is wound by an amazing, sacrificial love for the world.** Yes, God hates sin as much as he did in Old Testament times, but because of his incredible love, he wants to show mercy and wait just a little while longer. He wants to use that extra time to allow more people time to turn to Jesus Christ.

In the closing notes of "Naive," Chris Rice momentarily turns the questions away from God and directs them back to himself:

Am I naive?
Can I believe?
And can I leave in bigger hands?

Being human in a sinful world, each of us is naturally going to have tough questions that we want God to answer. But regardless of how God responds, a final question is aimed at you and you alone: can you simply believe and leave the universe in bigger hands? In the end, as Chris Rice helps show in "Naive," the big questions of life can only be answered with a heart of faith.

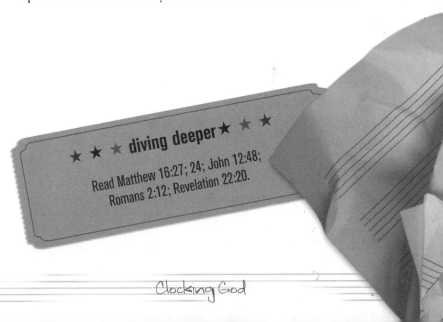

★ ★ ★ **diving deeper** ★ ★ ★
Read Matthew 16:27; 24; John 12:48; Romans 2:12; Revelation 22:20.

NAIVE
by Chris Rice

How long until You defend Your name
And set the record right?
How far will you allow the human race
To run and hide? Yeah
And how much can You tolerate our weaknesses
Before You step into our sky blue and say
"That's quite enough"?

[Chorus:]
Am I naive to want a remedy
For every bitter heart?
Can I believe You hold an
Exclamation point for every question mark? Yeah
And can I leave the timing of this universe
To bigger hands?
And may I be so bold to ask
You to please hurry?

I hear that a God who's good
Would never let the evil
Run so long
But I say it's because You're good
You're giving us more time
'Cause I believe that You love to show us mercy
But when will You step into our sky blue and say
"That's quite enough, and your time is up"? Yeah

[Repeat Chorus]

Am I naive?
Can I believe?
And can I leave in bigger hands?
And may I be so bold to ask You, to ask You,
To ask You
How long?

 ☐ See p. 263.

God's Boundless Love

Action Steps

In "Naive," Chris Rice deals with the impatience that we can have with God when we look at the bad things going on around us. As you wrestle with these issues, consider taking the following steps:

In a time of prayer, share openly with God your struggles with desiring immediate justice and answers.

When you start to get frustrated with God's timing, put on the brakes. Get your hands on a study Bible and, using the concordance, do a word study on "patience" throughout the Scriptures. Explore how God uses waiting to shape and mold us into the kind of people he wants us to be.

Pray that you will have the same motivation of love for the world as God does.

2

Faithful
to Our Harlots'
Hearts

Standing before a packed church on your wedding day, you gaze into the eyes of your spouse-to-be standing beside you at the altar. To the people watching from the pews, you two appear to be the perfect couple. A match made in heaven. Your close friends know all too well that this day is the fulfillment of a dream for you; for years now, they saw you wait patiently. You never gave up hope that your love would be returned by the one standing shoulder to shoulder with you now. And yet, despite the dreamy appearances, something is missing from your smile. Oh, it's not visible to those who look at you, not even to your future spouse. But behind your smiling facade is an aching, broken heart. **Today wasn't supposed to be like this,** you say to yourself.

Your thoughts drift back to that handwritten note you stumbled across the night before. Scrawled in the ink of betrayal, the letter told of your future spouse's plan to cheat on you soon after the honeymoon is over. Though you cried yourself to sleep last night, you were unwavering in your intention to go through with the wedding anyway. Your decision was not out of weakness but out of the depth of your love—even if that love was going to be spit upon by your "other half."

The echoing sound of "I do" suddenly jars you from your thoughts. The vows roll off the lips of your spouse-to-be so freely, almost as if they have no thought or conviction behind them. But when "for better or for worse" is spoken by the pastor, a small tear wells up in your eye as you strain to speak those sacred words "I do."

An outrageous scenario, you may say. After all, who would actually go through with a marriage ceremony knowing their future wife or husband was going to cheat on them? Yet this is what actually happened to an Old Testament prophet named Hosea who was told by God to marry an adulterous woman named Gomer. But the story of Hosea, sung about by Third Day in "Gomer's Theme," is not just about one man's broken heart. Far more importantly, the saga of this married couple serves as a striking parallel to the relationship between God and his people. This song puts to words both the depth of God's love for us and the heartbreak our sin causes him.

Unfaithful

While the Bible doesn't give all the details, we can imagine Hosea as a gentle, godly man who for years had a crush on a girl down the road named Gomer. She was drop-dead gorgeous, though perhaps always far more interested in the more muscular guys in town. But eventually Hosea wows Gomer and wins her heart, and she accepts his marriage proposal. As Third Day begins "Gomer's Theme," they express the joy and hope Hosea would have had as a young husband-to-be:

> In this place
> Saw her face
> He was more than happier
> Made for Him

Similarly, God has always had a special love like this for each and every person who has walked the earth. He created all humans in his perfect image yet singled out you as a one-of-a-kind. When God looks on your face, he is beyond happy. Or in the words of Third Day, he is "more than happier." In fact, you were "made for Him."

Back in the Old Testament days, God wanted to be thought of and treated as more than a "supreme being" who was far removed from humans living on planet Earth. So he decided to form a special marriage-like relationship with people who would commit to loving him. Early on, he established a covenant (agreement) between Abraham and himself. God promised that he would take care of Abraham and his descendants so long as they in return would obey him and stay away from sin. It seemed like a match made in heaven: a love affair between the Creator of the world and a group of people who would worship and obey the Lord their God of their own choosing.

And yet the covenant proved to be something right out of a bad afternoon soap opera. Yes, God always kept his end of the deal, but Abraham's descendents, the Israelites, never could. Just as the book of Hosea tells how Gomer cheated on Hosea, the Old Testament is filled with example after example of the Israelites' unfaithfulness to their God. Third Day sings of this betrayal as the first verse continues:

> It's a sin
> That she was not faithful
> She couldn't be
> Foolishly
> More unfaithful if she tried

Whatever Gomer's intentions were at the start of her marriage to Hosea, her love was fickle. Scripture describes it as being "like the morning mist, like the early dew that disappears" (Hosea 6:4). At some point after the wedding, Gomer began cheating on Hosea. Her sin wasn't just a one-night fling, either; it apparently became a regular, nasty habit. She ignored her vows and slept with other men, regardless of the hurt and pain that it caused her husband. The actions of Gomer seem outrageous, but her attitude expresses the same mockery that the Israelites made of their covenant relationship. They completely forgot their commitment to the Lord, lived as they pleased, and even worshiped other gods. Foolishly, like Gomer, they could not have been "more unfaithful if [they] tried."

Yet as sad as Hosea was because of Gomer's behavior, he was really not the least bit surprised. Perhaps he'd held out hope that it would not happen, but Hosea knew before he even married Gomer that she was going to cheat on him. God had told him that much. In the same way, God knew before the creation of the world that his people were going to be unfaithful to him. Yet in spite of that knowledge, he created them, loved them, and made a covenant with them.

Wandering Eyes

Hosea's love for Gomer was tough as nails. Not even her betrayal could kill it. As Third Day continues, they sing of this kind of love:

> He did not care
> Wanted her
> Despite lies and wandering eyes

Gomer's "lies and wandering eyes" were a continual slap in the face to her husband. And when we put our faith in our back pocket and live as we please, we are showing God that same kind of disregard and contempt. We become much like Gomer walking with her husband through the village market, all the while focusing her wandering eyes on other men as they walk past.

Amazingly, not only does Hosea look beyond this behavior, but his heart continues to be captivated by Gomer. As Third Day sings, Hosea "lavished on silver, gold, anything she needed." Yet these gifts are "wasted thoughts" on Gomer, because she does not appreciate or even acknowledge them.

As "Gomer's Theme" continues, Third Day contrasts how different Gomer and Hosea are because of what each does not remember. Gomer has forgotten all about her "first love," while Hosea has forgotten her betrayal and his broken heart. The lyrics put it like this:

> She's forgotten her first love
> (Maybe one day she'll return)
> He's forgotten that she ever
> Went away and broke His heart

As the song suggests, Gomer leaves Hosea. Feeling too constrained, she walks out on her husband and goes off to pursue her own selfish desires. The Bible is not specific about how much time passes, but at some point Hosea goes out to look for her. And when he does, Hosea finds his bride in the most miserable of circumstances: living as some kind of prostitute or slave. Instead of leaving her there to get the misery that she deserves, Hosea rescues her by buying her back from another man.

Too Late

The story of Hosea reveals just how remarkable God's love for his people is. However, in the final verse of "Gomer's Theme," Third Day offers a warning: God is not a pushover. While he continues to love us as we stray from him, don't wander too far; you may find it impossible to come back. Third Day sings:

> God only knows
> That He has shown her

More love than she deserves
There will come a time
When she will find
That He's not there
To give her love
And He'll be gone away
From her forever

Because of the free gift of grace that the New Testament promises, we can easily feel far removed and insulated from the Old Testament's judgments of fire and brimstone. As a result, we quite easily develop a casual attitude about our need to live a pure and holy life. When we are young, especially, we can believe that "living for Christ" is something to get serious about as we get older. To borrow words from a Blink 182 song, we can find ourselves asking God, "With many years ahead to fall in line, why would you wish that on me?"

But in "Gomer's Theme," Third Day reveals the problem with this kind of thinking: each of us has to respond to God's love within the time we have been given. At some point, your time is up. One day you may find that "He's not there" and "He'll be gone away . . . forever." Hosea 5:4 offers a scary warning: "Their deeds do not permit them to return to their God." In other words, your heart can become so hardened that you will never respond to Jesus's call again. The people of Israel found this out the hard way. As an illustration of his frustration with the Israelites, God instructs Hosea to name his third child a Hebrew name that means "not my people." In making this statement, God was rejecting the very people he desperately wanted to love. Much of the book of Hosea after this point is a series of judgments against the Israelites because of their Gomer-like unfaithfulness.

As real as that danger is, however, another reason we can't just put off our relationship with God is even more compelling: because in doing so, we completely misunderstand what the Christian life is all about. We start thinking of Christianity as a faith of "do's and don'ts," not as a marriage. But when our faith becomes following rules, we make God into a kind of cosmic high school principal—someone we have to obey to stay out of trouble, but not a person we would want to eat dinner with. Yet when we look at the love story of Gomer and Hosea, we can see that God has something far different in mind. God wants us to see him as a lover, someone who forms a marriage-like relationship with each of us. When we see God in that light, sin and disobedience have nothing to do with violating a list of rules and everything to do with breaking the heart of God.

The love story of Hosea and Gomer seems right out of the pages of a Shakespearean tragedy. But in spite of the betrayal and judgments, the book of Hosea contains an underlying message of hope. In fact, the name Hosea itself means "salvation." So as you listen to "Gomer's Theme" and read the book of Hosea in the Bible, remember God's heartfelt love note to you: return to him and he will heal your waywardness and love you freely (Hosea 14:4).

GOMER'S THEME
by Third Day

In this place
Saw her face
He was more than happier
Made for Him
It's a sin
That she was not faithful
She couldn't be
Foolishly
More unfaithful if she tried
He did not care
Wanted her
Despite lies and wandering eyes

He deserves the very best
But he loves her none the less

She's forgotten her first love
(Maybe one day she'll return)
He's forgotten that she ever
Went away and broke His heart

Lavished on
Silver, gold, anything she needed
Wasted thoughts
Broken hearts
Love was not acknowledged

God only knows
That He has shown her
More love than she deserves
There will come a time
When she will find
That He's not there
To give her love
And He'll be gone away
From her forever

Used by permission. [2]

★ ★ ★ **diving deeper** ★ ★ ★

Read the book of Hosea. Chapters 1–3 focus on the relationship between Gomer and Hosea. Chapters 4–14 center on God's judgments and restoration of Israel.

Read the story of the woman caught in the act of adultery in John 8:1–10 and see how Jesus, in spite of her being guilty as charged, showed her grace and mercy.

Action Steps

In "Gomer's Theme," Third Day puts to music the love story of Gomer and Hosea that is found in the book of Hosea. As you think about this song, personalize the story and see it as a description of your disobedience before the Lord. Once you do that, take the following steps:

Read chapters 1—3 in the book of Hosea. But as you do so, think of yourself as Gomer and Hosea as God. The reality of your sin will become clear to you in a new way as you read Hosea in this manner.

In a time of prayer, confess your past sin and disobedience and acknowledge all of the things that God has done for you.

Strive to be holy and walk in God's ways. The book of Hosea is a picture of the consequences of disobedience and unfaithfulness. Don't make the same mistakes that the Israelites did.

Challenge yourself with the two questions that close the book of Hosea: "Who is wise?" and "Who is discerning?" (14:9) Write down three specific steps you can take in your life to gain wisdom and discernment.

God's Boundless Love

3

Mind the Gap

If you go to London and travel on the Underground subway, you'll see signs telling you to "mind the gap." That's the British way of saying "pay attention" when boarding the subway—don't get your foot stuck in the space between the train and the platform.

We can deal with that sort of gap through ordinary common sense, but other gaps in life are far more challenging. They require hard work and perseverance to overcome. People throughout history have always been driven to conquer these great divides—between where they are today and what is possible tomorrow. The New World discovered. Everest climbed. The South Pole traversed. The moon trodden. In fact, we have been so successful at overcoming gaps that real life resembles a line in *The Truman Show*. A young Truman tells his teacher that he wants to be another Magellan. Dousing his hopes, she responds, "Oh, you're too late! There's nothing left to explore!" Indeed, humans seem to have no more challenges left to conquer on this planet.

One gap, however, humans will never be able to overcome. Not with common sense or hard work or technology. I am talking about the rift between the holiness of God and the sinfulness of man. No amount of human sweat can ever bring those two extremes together. In fact, as you grow more holy and Christlike as you live your life, you will find the distance never seems to shrink. It actually grows! That's because the closer you get to God, the more clearly your eyes will see how truly awesome God is and how insignificant your efforts are in comparison.

This gap between God and man was the inspiration for Jars of Clay to write "Hymn." Through this song we can see that God, in his infinite greatness, forms a bridge between man and

One gap humans will never be able to overcome. Not with common sense or hard work or technology.

himself. As Jars of Clay sings about, the only action required on our part is to "mind the gap" and worship him.

Looking Ahead

As "Hymn" begins, Jars of Clay contrasts both sides of the great divide—the awesome glory and love of God and the weak nature of man. The first verse goes like this:

> Oh refuge of my hardened heart
> Oh fast pursuing lover come
> As angels dance around Your throne
> My life by captured fare You own

This verse echoes Psalm 46:1, a promise that God is our refuge and strength. Psalm 57:1 adds that, like a baby bird finds safety under its mother, we can take refuge in the shadow of the Lord's wings. This safe haven is not just an exclusive club for really good people—the Mother Teresas or Billy Grahams of the world. No, God even offers safety for my "hardened heart," regardless of what I have done in the past. Because of God's grace, I don't have to measure up to any standard before he'll take me in. If I willingly go to him, he will provide refuge.

God is not stingy about offering this kind of love for you either. In fact, Jars of Clay calls the Lord your "fast pursuing lover." He hunts you with a startling intensity. Jesus tells us as much in the parable of the prodigal son (see Luke 15:11–32). When the prodigal returns home in desperation after screwing up his life, his father sees him far off and is "filled with compassion for him" (v. 20).

It's easy to gloss over the term *compassion* in English, but the actual Greek word originally used is emotionally charged, having as its root "innards" or "intestines." You see, in Jesus's day, people thought of emotions as being centered in the stomach or abdomen. Author Kenneth Bailey discovered that even today, when someone in the Middle East hears a sad story, a common expression translates as "You are cutting up my intestines." In this parable, then, Jesus is saying in effect that the father's "intestines were all cut up" in concern for his son. So the father cannot sit idly by, waiting for the prodigal to walk up the road. Instead, like a "fast pursuing lover," the father sprints off as fast as he can to greet his son far down the pathway before their house.

Jesus's calls to discipleship . . . emerge as the only response to God's greatness and love that make sense.

This gut-wrenching love motivated God to come to the earth as Jesus Christ. He paid the "captured fare" in full for us, taking the punishment for our sins on himself when he died on the cross. As a result of this act, our debt to God is so great that one fact should be just plain obvious: he owns us. Or, as Jars of Clay says, "My life by captured fare you own." Seen in this light, Jesus's calls to discipleship—"Die to yourself" and "Take up your cross"—not only seem proper but emerge as the only response to God's greatness and love that makes sense.

While God may "own" our lives, we never need to feel like our hands are tied. His refuge and love actually provide us with the ultimate freedom. Fear and worry are outdated, so "last year." We no longer have anything to sweat over. As the apostle Paul says in Romans 8:31, when God is for us, who can ever be against us? Jars of Clay expresses this truth as the song continues:

Not silhouette of trodden faith
Nor death shall not my steps be guide
I'll pirouette upon mine grave
For in Your path I'll run and hide

When we allow God to own our lives, our time on earth will never become "a silhouette of trodden faith"—an image of a defeated, worn-out trust. Instead, as we surrender to Christ, God begins to transform us from the inside out. Any hardness that we started with will begin to fall off piece by piece, much like a snake shedding its skin. The impact of God's power and love will become more and more obvious in our lives, allowing us to escape from fear and worry.

Even the thing that every person instinctively fears most—death—no longer has power over us when we take refuge in God. Jars of Clay sings, "Death shall not my steps be guide." In other words, death no longer dictates our future. Instead, it becomes just the doorway to experiencing the fullness of God when we join him in heaven. Our hope in Christ is so true and real, we can even "pirouette"—do a ballet twirl—on our grave. If you are a Christian, that is not just keeping a "stiff upper lip" and trying to act casual in the face of danger. That is genuine Christian truth!

In his poem "Prospice," Robert Browning reflects this same confidence that Christians have over death's grip. He writes, "For sudden the worst turns the best to the brave." When death and tragedy come our way, what initially seems like the worst thing imaginable is actually the best thing that can happen to Christians who persevere. Paul echoes this Christian truth in what is surely one of the most eloquent lines in all of Scripture, 1 Corinthians 15:55: "Where, O death, is your victory? Where, O death, is your sting?" Medieval poet John Donne chimes in, adding, "Death, thou shalt die." When we begin to live in the reality of Christ's hope, our perspective will begin to resemble that of Robert Browning, the apostle Paul, and John Donne: death itself is no longer a scary business. That hope allows us to join Jars of Clay in singing with confidence, "In Your path I'll run and hide."

As "Hymn" continues in the third verse, Jars of Clay sings about the glory and victory that lie beyond death for those who trust in God. Heaven will "break the spell of pain" that despair and tragedy spin in our lives today. What's more, since Revelation 21:4 promises there will be no more death or sorrow or mourning or pain, "the bludgeoned heart shall burst in vain." The poison arrows of Satan will no longer be able to penetrate and break our hearts. Instead, God's love and truth will rule forever in that future glory.

However, while that promise to come is guaranteed, it can seem so far away when we have to deal with the harsh realities of the here and now. So in the final verse of "Hymn," Jars of Clay asks Jesus Christ to protect me and be my desire throughout this earthly life:

> Sweet Jesus carry me away
> From cold of night and dust of day
> In ragged hour or salt worn eye
> Be my desire, my well sprung lye

Let Jesus Christ be your Savior from the extremes of life, from the "cold of night" to the "dust of day." And during the "ragged hour" in which you face hardship, allow Jesus to be your desire, the thing you want most out of life. When your "salt worn eye" is tired from heartache, simply let Jesus be your "well sprung lye," your source for life and purity.

Springing Worship

When we "mind the gap" and begin to live out life in the shadow of God's love, our selfishness and pride will be transformed. Jars of Clay sings about this truth in the chorus of "Hymn":

Oh gaze of love so melt my pride
That I may in Your house but kneel
And in my brokenness to cry
Spring worship unto Thee

Here Jars of Clay illustrates why worship is so natural when we recognize that we can do nothing on our own to get into God's good graces. As we accept God's love, he begins to melt our pride and take our self-centeredness away. Genuine humility and brokenness are produced inside us. And as we begin to better grasp God's holiness, we cannot help but kneel and worship our Lord and Savior—to "spring worship unto Thee."

Over the years Jars of Clay has routinely closed its concerts with "Hymn." They do so because when listeners consider this gap between the awesomeness of God and the weakness of man, they quickly take their adoring eyes off of the band itself and fix them squarely on Jesus Christ.

God desires to be your fast pursuing lover. He longs to draw you into the shadow of his wings. "It is up to God, after all, to have us," wrote poet Rainer Maria Rilke. "Our part consists of almost solely in letting him grasp us."[1] So mind the gap. Let God catch you. And spring worship unto him.

HYMN
by Jars of Clay

Oh refuge of my hardened heart
Oh fast pursuing lover come
As angels dance 'round Your throne
My life by captured fare You own

Not silhouette of trodden faith
Nor death shall not my steps be guide
I'll pirouette upon mine grave
For in Your path I'll run and hide

[Chorus:]
Oh gaze of love so melt my pride
That I may in Your house but kneel
And in my brokenness to cry
Spring worship unto Thee

When beauty breaks the spell of pain
The bludgeoned heart shall burst in vain
But not when love be pointed king
And truth shall Thee forever reign

[Chorus]

Sweet Jesus carry me away
From cold of night and dust of day
In ragged hour or salt worn eye
Be my desire, my well sprung lye

[Repeat Chorus]

Spring worship unto Thee
Spring worship unto Thee

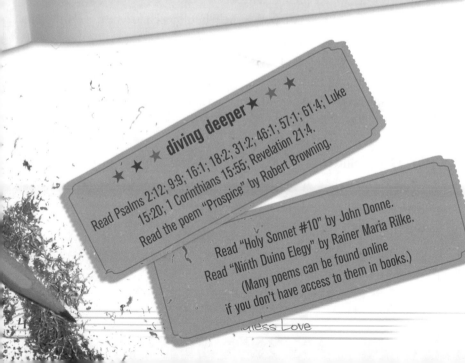

★ ★ ★ diving deeper ★ ★ ★

Read Psalms 2:12; 9:9; 16:1; 18:2; 31:2; 46:1; 57:1; 61:4; Luke
15:20; 1 Corinthians 15:55; Revelation 21:4.
Read the poem "Prospice" by Robert Browning.

Read "Holy Sonnet #10" by John Donne.
Read "Ninth Duino Elegy" by Rainer Maria Rilke.
(Many poems can be found online
if you don't have access to them in books.)

Action Steps

In "Hymn," Jars of Clay sings about the great divide between the greatness of God and the corruption of man. Yet when you surrender to God, he will gladly be your refuge and your fast pursuing lover for all eternity. As you reflect on these truths, consider the following steps:

Eternal security, joy, and love come to those who give their lives to Jesus Christ. If you have not already done so, commit your life to Jesus Christ and hand over the keys of your life to him.

Draw one circle on each end of a piece of paper. Label one "God" and the other "me." In the middle, write down the sins in your life that get in the way of a relationship with God. Now, to represent that God is the one who bridges the distance between you and himself, draw an arrow from God's circle—over the sin—to your own and label it with a cross. Remember that God "minded the gap" out of love, not because of anything you did. Finally, after you offer a prayer of thanksgiving for God's grace, rip up the paper as a symbol of the fact that God wipes away those sins that came between you and him.

Next Sunday, enter your church's worship service in a spirit of brokenness and thanksgiving for God's all-pursuing love. The best way to do this is to take some time alone to reflect and pray before walking through the doors of your church.

Focus on the "gap" in your quiet time for a week. Study one of the following chapters in the book of Psalms for each day of the week: Psalm 2; 9; 16; 18; 31; 46; and 61.

Part Two

Freedom
and
Iden

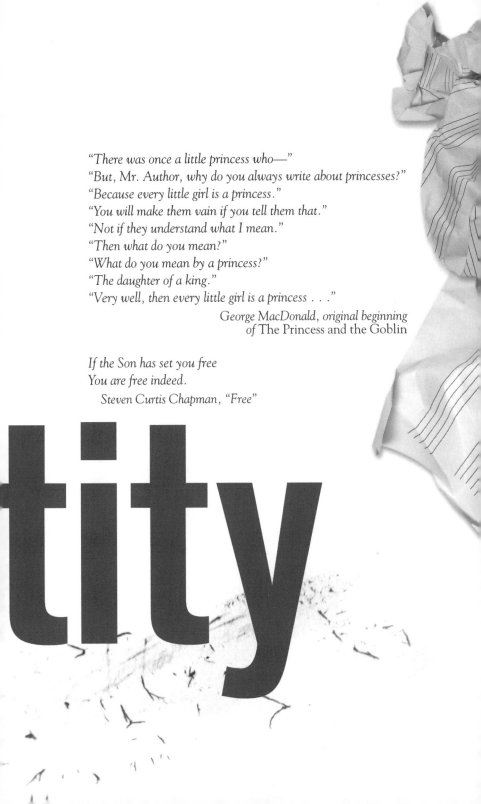

"There was once a little princess who—"
"But, Mr. Author, why do you always write about princesses?"
"Because every little girl is a princess."
"You will make them vain if you tell them that."
"Not if they understand what I mean."
"Then what do you mean?"
"What do you mean by a princess?"
"The daughter of a king."
"Very well, then every little girl is a princess . . ."

George MacDonald, *original beginning
of* The Princess and the Goblin

*If the Son has set you free
You are free indeed.*
   Steven Curtis Chapman, *"Free"*

tity

4

Get Busy Living

People live in all sorts of prisons. Some are made with brick and mortar and are surrounded by razor-wire fences. Others are spiritual in nature and found buried deep within a person's soul. Living inside either of these prisons year after year deadens a person and slowly sucks his life away. The 1994 film *The Shawshank Redemption* throws a light on how this can happen.[1] The film tells the story of Andy Dufresne, a young, fast-rising banker who is convicted of murder and sentenced to life in prison. As the years pass by, Andy gets to know Brooks, an older man who has lived all of his adult life inside the penitentiary. During the course of his lifetime, prison had become part of who he was, so much so that when paroled, he cannot handle living in the outside world. Not long after his release, Brooks ends up taking his own life. Reflecting on this tragedy, Andy's best friend in prison, Red, speaks about the long-term effect of the prison walls:

> These walls are funny. First you hate 'em. Then you get used to 'em. Enough time passes, you get so you depend on them. That's institutionalized. . . . They send you here for life; that's exactly what they take. The part that counts, anyway.[2]

While Red is speaking of the kind of prison walls that he can see and touch, the walls of sin act exactly the same way. At first you hate being a slave to sin. But as you continue sinning more and more, you get used to it. And if enough time passes, you can become "institutionalized" in sin and actually begin to depend on those walls. When this happens, sin carves out a home in your heart and stakes a claim on your soul.

Yet, as Jesus says in John 8, **life does not have to be this way.** His whole purpose for coming to earth and dying on the cross was to set us free. Free from the bondage of sin. Free from being "institutionalized" inside sin's walls. Real freedom, no matter the circumstances or surroundings we find ourselves in today. In his song "Free," Steven Curtis Chapman sings about how we can escape these prison walls and experience the lasting freedom that can only be found in Christ.

Harmonicas

"Free" was written by Chapman after he began visiting prisons and working with Prison Fellowship ministry. His personal experience in prison ministry, he says, enabled him to see the power of God's grace in ways he never could before. As Chapman begins "Free," he describes the intimidating and downright scary experience of entering a penitentiary:

The sun was beating down inside the walls of stone and razor wire
As we made our way across the prison yard
I felt my heart begin to race as we drew nearer to the place
Where they say that death is waiting in the dark
The slamming doors of iron echoed through the halls
Where despair holds life within its cruel claws

From Chapman's description, we can imagine how hopelessness would run wild inside a place like that. The despair of being surrounded 24/7 by ugly stone walls and razor wire. The gloom of living next to others who have let sin put a stranglehold on their lives. In this world, hope becomes a four-letter word, a cruel hoax best ignored. "Hope is a dangerous thing," says Red in *The Shawshank Redemption*. "Hope can drive a man insane."[3] Whether we are an inmate in a maximum-security prison or a prisoner to the sin inside us, our world can take on that same hopelessness and despair. Like Red, we can start to see life as somehow easier to deal with if we throw away any chance of hope or escape.

Yet no matter how bleak our circumstances are, Christ offers a way out. And in the midst of a scene of hopelessness, Steven Curtis Chapman makes an amazing discovery—a seed of hope in this dark, despairing world.

> But then I met a man whose face seemed so
>   strangely out of place
> A blinding light of hope was shining in his eyes
> And with repentance in his voice he told me of
>   his tragic choice
> That led him to this place where he must pay
>   the price
> But then his voice grew strong as he began to
>   tell
> About the One he said had rescued him from
>   hell, he said. . .

This prisoner had every reason to be "institutionalized," as resistant to hope as Red was. Yet the man had a "blinding light of hope . . . shining in his eyes." He knew that no matter what his temporary surroundings were, he had been rescued from hell.

Because he was saved by Jesus Christ, the man had the assurance of an eternity that would wash away all of his temporary, earthly sin and pain.

Chuck Colson, author and founder of Prison Fellowship, tells in his book *The Body* the true story of Hanani Mikhalovich, who faced a different sort of "prison." Hanani was a major in the army of the former Soviet Union. As an up-and-coming young leader in the Red Army, he heard the gospel through a missionary radio broadcast. Not long after, Hanani committed his life to Jesus Christ, an unspeakable deed for anyone with ambition in the atheistic Soviet government. In the weeks that followed, his superiors soon noticed that a major change had taken place in Hanani. When asked, Hanani openly discussed his newfound faith and that his primary allegiance was to Jesus Christ, not the motherland.

His superiors were furious and planned to do something about it. Word quickly spread on the army base that a special ceremony was going to be held on the military parade grounds. Local citizens were even encouraged to attend. At the time of the ceremony, the crowd arrived, the troops marched in, and the band played. Then, when everyone was at attention, Hanani heard his name called over the loudspeaker and was asked to come forward.

When you commit your life to Jesus Christ, your spirit cannot be touched by sin or Satan.

Hanani made his way to the front of the crowd and stood at attention. A communist official began ranting and raving over Hanani's betrayal of the country. Hanani's commanding officer then ripped the stripes and medals from Hanani's jacket and threw his hat to the ground. He was then led around in front of the stands with people laughing and mocking him. The spectacle proved too much for his wife. She would leave soon after to escape the shame.

The last act of humiliation came when Hanani's superior handed him a broom and demoted him to the job of a janitor. This janitorial job would end up being the only career that this once fast-rising young star would ever know, a job Hanani held until he was seventy.[4]

The Christian prisoner Steven Curtis Chapman sings about and Hanani Mikhalovich were imprisoned for far different reasons—the prisoner because of his "tragic choice," while Hanani simply for his beliefs. Regardless, both men accepted their circumstances and kept their faith in the midst of hardship. Neither man focused on how bad he had it. Instead, each had an infectious smile and a "blinding light of hope" shining in his eyes.

In *The Shawshank Redemption*, this kind of hope is expressed through music. When Andy starts talking about the power of music, Red reveals that he played the harmonica in his youth but gave it up because it seemed pointless to play in prison. Andy counters:

> Here's where it makes the most sense. You need it so you don't forget. . . . Forget that there are places in the world that aren't made out of stone. That there's a—there's something inside that they can't get to, that they can't touch. That's yours.[5]

Think of the Bible as your harmonica, so to speak. God's Word reminds you that when you commit your life to Jesus Christ, your spirit cannot be touched by sin or Satan, no matter what circumstances you find yourself in.

Timeless Freedom

The chorus of "Free" speaks of the reason for this hope: the freedom that every Christian has in Christ. John 8:35–36 says

Freedom and Identity

that Christ sets us free from our sins and gives us assurance of eternal life with him. Our chains of sin have been taken off, and we have been given wings to fly above all the smut and stains. Chapman sings:

I'm free, yeah, oh, I have been forgiven
God's love has taken off my chains and given me these wings
And I'm free, yeah, yeah, and the freedom I've been given
Is something that not even death can take away from me
Because I'm free
Jesus set me free

This freedom in Christ does not mean that we will live sin-free lives. But it does mean that sin can't hold us down without our permission, that we are freed from the shackles of sin, despair, and hopelessness. The apostle Paul calls Christians "the Lord's freedmen," indicating the spiritual freedom that Christians have in the past, present, and future. What does that freedom mean to you?

First, you are freed from all sins you ever committed in the past. God's grace is unlimited. Whether we sinned once or a million times, whether we told a white lie or committed a heinous crime—no matter. When we come to God and ask for forgiveness, he is faithful and just and will forgive our sins (1 John 1:9). What's more, our sins are forgotten by God and will never be held against us (Ps. 103:12; Jer. 31:34).

Second, you are freed from any longer being a slave to your sins. Paul writes in Romans 6:6–7 that the old, sinful you was crucified with Jesus on the cross "so that the body of sin might be done away with, that we should no longer be slaves to sin." The word *slavery* has perhaps lost its sting slightly in modern times because its horrors are confined to history books rather than being something we actually see occurring before our eyes. However, since slavery was a reality throughout the Roman Empire, Paul's original readers would know exactly what he meant. Being a "slave to sin" means that you are in bondage against your will, being utterly controlled and dominated by your sinful nature inside of you. Paul goes on to say that when we die with Christ, it doesn't make sense at all that we could be a slave to sin—because anyone who has died has been freed from these shackles.

Third, you are free to experience eternity with Jesus Christ. When you become a Christian, you immediately become bought and paid for by Christ. You are freed from the chains of hell and are guaranteed a place with God throughout eternity.

Gentle Slopes

As "Free" continues in the second verse, Chapman shares his experience leaving the prison:

We said a prayer and said good-bye and tears
began to fill my eyes
As I stepped back out into the blinding sun
And even as I drove away I found that I
could not escape
The way he spoke of what the grace of God
had done
I thought about how sin had sentenced us to
die
And how God gave His only Son so you and I
could say . . .

Chapman realizes that "sin had sentenced us to die." He emphasizes "us," not just the prisoner. The only difference is that the prisoner can easily see the obvious, painful consequences of his sin, while our sin is often much easier to gloss over to the outside world. In fact, modern culture even approves of and encourages many sins, making it harder for us to realize our need for freedom. And that's just the way Satan likes it. C. S. Lewis points out in *The Screwtape Letters* that from Satan's perspective, "murder is no better than cards if cards will do the trick. . . . Indeed, the [most dangerous] road to hell is the gradual one—the gentle slope . . . without milestones, without signposts."[6] Chapman's experience in the prison reminded him of the fact that each of us, apart from Christ, has the same curse of sin upon us as a death-row inmate does.

Free Indeed

Chapman once shared that his most unforgettable memory of "Free" occurred before the song even came out on his *Signs of Life* CD. He was performing the song in a maximum-security prison in South Carolina. During the last chorus, all of the inmates there rose to their feet and began to applaud, fighting unsuccessfully to hold back tears. Recalls Chapman, "It was a very profound experience of the presence of God and the reality of this song."[7] This reality of God's promise is made crystal clear in the last line of the bridge of "Free":

> Oh, if the Son has set you free
> Then you are free, really, really free

Toward the closing of *The Shawshank Redemption*, Red is finally paroled from prison. Now in his sixties, institutionalized himself after decades of being imprisoned, he starts out following a similar path as the old man Brooks did years before. Yet before he repeats the same fate as Brooks, Red determines to fulfill a promise he'd made to Andy some time back. Red had agreed that if he were ever released, he'd travel to a farm in rural Maine and dig up a box that was buried under a certain rock there. Clinging to that promise, Red makes that visit, and the contents of that box give Red the hope that he yearned for. In the process he realizes that he can choose whether or not to accept his newfound freedom. He reflects:

> Get busy living, or get busy dying. . . . I find I'm so excited I can barely sit still or hold a thought in my head. I think it's the excitement only a free man can feel. A free man at the start of a long journey, whose conclusion is uncertain. I hope I can make it across the border. I hope to see my friend and shake his hand. I hope the Pacific is as blue as it has been in my dreams. I hope . . .[8]

FREE
by Steven Curtis Chapman

The sun was beating down inside the walls
of stone and razor wire
As we made our way across the prison yard
I felt my heart begin to race as we drew
nearer to the place
Where they say that death is waiting in the
dark
The slamming doors of iron echoed
through the halls
Where despair holds life within its cruel
claws
But then I met a man whose face seemed so
strangely out of place
A blinding light of hope was shining in his
eyes
And with repentance in his voice he told
me of his tragic choice
That led him to this place where he must
pay the price
But then his voice grew strong as he began
to tell
About the One he said had rescued him
from hell, he said . . .

[Chorus:]
I'm free, yeah, oh, I have been forgiven
God's love has taken off my chains and
given me these wings
And I'm free, yeah, yeah, and the freedom
I've been given
Is something that not even death can take
away from me
Because I'm free
Jesus set me free

We said a prayer and said good-bye and
tears began to fill my eyes
As I stepped back out into the blinding sun
And even as I drove away I found that I
could not escape
The way he spoke of what the grace of God
had done
I thought about how sin had sentenced us to
die
And how God gave His only Son so you and
I could say . . .

Like Red, Hanani Mikhalovich, and the Christian prisoner, you have a choice—get busy living, or get busy dying. Claim the freedom you have in Christ and get busy living today.

If the Son has set you free
You are free indeed

[Chorus]

And if the Son has set you free
Oh, if the Son has set you free
Then you are free indeed
Oh, you are really free
If the Son has set you free
Oh, if the Son has set you free
Then you are free, really, really free

Oh, we're free yeah, oh, we have been forgiven
God's grace has broken every chain and given us these wings
And we're free, yeah, yeah, and the freedom we've been given
Is something that not even death can take from you and me
Because we're free, yeah, the freedom we've been given
Is something that not even death can take from you and me
Because we're free, oh, we're free
We are free, we are free
The Son has set us free

Action Steps

Steven Curtis Chapman sings in "Free" about the true freedom you can experience through Jesus Christ. Whether you are imprisoned inside stone walls or the walls of sin, consider the following action steps:

Prayerfully examine yourself to see if sin has you trapped inside any prison walls. Experience true freedom in Christ by giving your life to him today.

Get involved with a prison ministry. Pray about going to prisons to work with prisoners directly or supporting prison ministries in other ways. Reaching out to prisoners is an important command. Jesus even speaks specifically of this activity in Matthew 25:31–46.

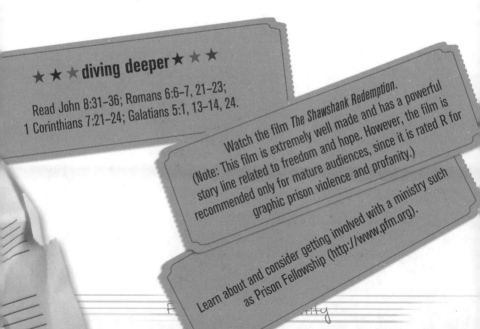

★ ★ ★ **diving deeper** ★ ★ ★

Read John 8:31–36; Romans 6:6–7, 21–23; 1 Corinthians 7:21–24; Galatians 5:1, 13–14, 24.

Watch the film *The Shawshank Redemption*. (Note: This film is extremely well made and has a powerful story line related to freedom and hope. However, the film is recommended only for mature audiences, since it is rated R for graphic prison violence and profanity.)

Learn about and consider getting involved with a ministry such as Prison Fellowship (http://www.pfm.org).

5

A New Life

You ain't no kind of man if you ain't got land.

Delmar, O Brother, Where Art Thou?

"You ain't no kind of man if you ain't got land." While that line was spoken softly in the film O *Brother, Where Art Thou?* I suspect the same sentiment was screaming in the hearts of African-American slaves in the nineteenth-century United States. Slaves were forced to labor in the fields from sunrise to sunset. They worked on land that they did not own to harvest a crop they would receive no share in. Every part of their lives—their freedom, self-esteem, and chance at farming for themselves—was put in shackles.

However, after the Civil War ended and the slaves were liberated, some of these newly freed slaves had their dreams fulfilled with "forty acres and a mule." As a way of offering a fresh start, the government provided a grant to a number of freed slaves: they would receive forty acres of farmland and a mule that could be used to plow and till it. Sadly, not all former slaves got this offer, but those who did received an opportunity they could hardly have imagined possible a few years before. A freed slave went from feeling like "no kind of man" as he sweated over another's land to experiencing the joy of a brand-new beginning—farming on his *own* small piece of earth.

God's land of redemption is calling out for you

Using the vivid "forty acres and a mule" imagery, Caedmon's Call sings in "40 Acres" about the opportunity that every person has to be a "freed slave"—released from the shackles of sin and guilt—and begin a new life in Jesus Christ. God's land of redemption is calling out for you, says Caedmon's Call. All you have to do is get on the highway and come to him.

Go West, Young Man

The American West has always captured the hearts and imaginations of Americans. Ever since the days of Lewis and Clark, the West has signified adventure, spectacular beauty, and unlimited opportunity. Texas in particular was a favorite destination for many of the early settlers. Some who were unable to find work in the eastern cities or buy affordable farmland elsewhere headed to Texas to make a new life for themselves. Others arrived on the state line with a tarnished past, simply hoping for a place where they could start over. And, yes, even some of the newly freed slaves went there to farm. The monster size of Texas on any United States map was matched only by the giant-sized opportunities that were there for the taking.

This sense of "bigness" carries over to today when people think of the Lone Star State. Take a road trip out to Interstate 40 in western Texas and head toward New Mexico, and you will get a quick lesson in just how big Texas is. Not only does the highway seem to go on straight into eternity, but you'll be convinced that you can see forever in every direction. As "40 Acres" begins, Caedmon's Call sings about this vastness of the Texas plains:

> Out on these Texas plains you can see for a million lives
> And there's a thousand exits between here and the state line

Just as the apostle Paul speaks of "incomparable riches" (Eph. 2:4–9), Caedmon's Call uses Texas to symbolize the amazing size of God's grace and mercy. In fact, as we speak to others who have been transformed by Jesus Christ, we can begin to "see for a million lives" just how great his grace really is.

When we are enslaved in a life of sin, however, that promise can seem like a million miles away. We can feel totally defeated, or as "40 Acres" says,

> About the last time that I saw you
> You said call me Pandora, call me a fool

Our past easily becomes baggage that makes it difficult to turn to Jesus Christ. Guilt, shame, and regret can weigh us down so much that we just want to give up. Perhaps we start to believe that our sins are so terrible that God can never forgive us. Or perhaps we doubt whether Jesus even has the power to free us from our bondage. We can start to feel, as Caedmon's Call says, like Pandora. According to Greek mythology, Pandora was given a box as a present by the god Zeus, but she was forbidden from ever opening it. You guessed it: curiosity eventually got the better of Pandora, and she opened the box. As she did so, evil, disease, and despair escaped and spread out across the entire world. Much the same way, we may look back on our lives and cry out in frustration, "Call me Pandora." Decisions that seemed minor at the time unleashed consequences that were far worse than we could have ever imagined.

As "40 Acres" continues in the second verse, Caedmon's Call once again contrasts God's Texas-sized grace with our feelings of smallness and helplessness. Like the Texas sky, God's love and mercy never end. But while God's grace may be "as big as the sea," that promise can seem an ocean away when we are stuck in the midst of sin. Caedmon's Call puts it like this:

> Out here the Texas sky is as big as the sea
> And you're alone in your room like an island
> floating free
> Your spirit's hanging in a bottle out on a tree
> You say that you're the black sheep, I say
> you're still family

This verse highlights the sense of defeat we can feel when living a life of sin apart from God. Alone. Like an outcast. And forever trapped in our sins.

The heart of all sin is selfishness and pride. That's why when we sin, we drive a wedge between ourselves and God. After a while, we can start to feel all alone, like "an island floating free," lost in an empty sea and miles away from the shores of help. This distance that we have created between God and ourselves makes us feel like an outcast, like a "black sheep" that does not belong anywhere near God.

This sense of isolation spurs on a kind of claustrophobia: we feel trapped and unable to break free from our situation. Caedmon's Call brings this to mind when they sing, "Your spirit's hanging in a bottle out on a tree," a reference to a classic fairy tale called *Spirit in a Bottle*. In the story, a spirit is tricked into going into a glass bottle and is unable to get out unless someone comes along and releases him. Similarly, when we are living apart from God, we can feel duped by Satan into a bottle of sin and trapped in there, unable to come out.

Decision Time

Caedmon's Call begins each verse of "40 Acres" with an image that brings to mind God's incomparable grace, then acknowledges the barriers we may raise that prevent us from receiving that gift. They then close each verse with a challenge:

Drop these scales and take a look. The first verse urges us to wipe away the sin from our eyes and look to God. The apostle Paul became a Christian after being struck blind by a vision of the resurrected Jesus Christ. Paul was healed of his blindness a few days later; at the time of his healing, "something like scales" fell from his eyes, and he was able to see again (see Acts 9:1–19). Caedmon's Call tells us to do as Paul did: "Drop these scales and take a look." When we let our sin and past drop from our eyes, we'll see the beauty of God's forgiveness.

Throw that bottle to the waves. When we are feeling isolated and trapped like that spirit inside the bottle, the second verse challenges us to "throw that bottle to the waves." As we do so, Jesus Christ promises that the waves will "bring you in to me and from the shore you will see," as Caedmon's Call puts it. Jesus will open that bottle and release you from captivity.

Both verses leave us with the same challenge and a promise: release your sin into God's hands, and you'll see firsthand a new life waiting there for you.

Redemption

Imagine, for a moment, what one of those freed slaves must have felt as he and his family began their new life together in freedom. For decades this man would have known nothing but the hopeless, miserable life of slavery. He had probably resigned himself to the fact that he'd die being owned by another man. Yet after a flurry of events this man finds himself not only free but also a farmer with his own plot of land. As he holds the title of his land in his hands for the first time, I imagine that he can't help but smile from ear to ear. He glances down at the piece of paper and begins to bubble over with laughter. He gently nudges his wife, telling her to look at his name written in ink on the deed. After a few moments he tries to put it down, but he can't bring himself to do so. He just enjoys a look at the deed again, all the while laughing in joy.

As incredible as this experience was for those freed slaves, their happiness was hollow compared to the joy that we can receive in Jesus Christ. The chorus of "40 Acres" describes Christ's wonderful promise to each of us:

There's forty acres and redemption to be
found
Just along down the way
There is a place where no plow blade has
turned the ground
And you will turn it over, 'cause out here hope
remains
'Cause out here hope remains . . .

When we come to Christ, we will find "forty acres and redemption" waiting for us. Jesus says in John 8:34–36, "Everyone who sins is a slave to sin. . . . So if the Son sets you free, you will be free indeed." As Jesus unshackles our chains, however, he doesn't just give us a second-rate farm in their place. Instead, our forty acres are virgin land, "a place where no plow blade has turned the ground." Your new life is indeed a clean slate. Your sins are as far away from you as the east is from the west. You are considered holy, "without blemish and free from accusation," according to Colossians 1:22.

After we receive Christ's redemption, we can experience the reality of a true hope, a hope we could only hunger for when we were held captive. We can read real-life stories of slaves in the American South or prisoners in concentration camps during World War II. In every case, hope was the common ingredient for the survivors of those ordeals. With hope, we can live through a lot of pain and suffering. But without it, we throw up our arms and die. Not only is this true when we are physically held captive, but it is especially true when we are in the spiritual bondage of sin. Without Christ, there's no hope. But as Caedmon's Call sings, when we are in the presence of Christ, "out here hope remains."

Poet William Wordsworth once said, "Hope rules a land for ever green." For Christians, that is more than a sweet line of poetry; it is livable truth. You can take it to the bank. The hope that you have in Christ will never be taken away and will rule your forty acres forever green.

After the Rains

While we will experience freedom and assurance in Christ's redemption, the song's final verse reminds us that new life as a Christian isn't always going to be easy. The verse starts out with this:

Out here the Texas rain is the hardest I've ever seen

It'll wash your house away, but it'll also make you clean

Think back to the freed slaves after they started toiling their land. Their new life as struggling farmers would not have been easy. In fact, I imagine it would have been quite difficult; they probably found themselves working longer hours and dealing with more challenges than ever before. But you can be certain that to a man, no freed slave would have exchanged those hardships for the chains of their former lives.

In the same way, living out the Christian faith can be hard stuff. God's "Texas rain is the hardest" you will experience. His floodwaters will rage and "wash your house away." But Christ does this for a single purpose: to remove the mud stains of sin in our lives and mold us into the people God created us to be.

To close the last verse of "40 Acres," Caedmon's Call offers one last invitation:

Now these rocks they are crying too
And this whole land is calling out for you

When Jesus rode into Jerusalem on a donkey on Palm Sunday, the people of the city cried out "Hosanna!" claiming him as Messiah. Outraged, the Pharisees commanded Jesus to shut the people up. Jesus responded by saying that even if the people were quiet, the "stones will cry out" (see Luke 19:37–40). In the same way, God's message of grace and forgiveness is so undeniable that the word just has to get out—the rocks "are crying too" and "this whole land is calling out for you."

In the film *O Brother, Where Art Thou?* Delmar is one of a trio of fugitives who go on an odyssey in search of a buried treasure.

When asked what he is going to do with his share of the loot, Delmar shares with his two friends the painful story of how he went bankrupt and lost his farm. Since that time, his hope and motivation have always been to buy the farm back from the bank. Not willing to even consider an alternative, he says, "You ain't no kind of man if you ain't got land."

In the end, whether you have property or farmland in this life matters nothing in light of eternity. But when you consider a certain forty-acre plot that Jesus has waiting for you, then Delmar's statement does ring true. If you ain't got *his* land, you ain't got nothing. Come get your forty acres and experience the redemption and hope that Christ alone can offer.

★★★ diving deeper ★★★

Read Psalms 103:12; John 8:34–36; Acts 9:1–19; 2 Corinthians 12:7–10; Ephesians 2:7; Colossians 1:22; 1 Peter 1:6–7.

40 ACRES
by Caedmon's Call

Out on these Texas plains you can see for a
million lives
And there's a thousand exits between here
and the state line
About the last time that I saw you
You said call me Pandora, call me a fool
And I'm thinking this view it could do you
some good
So drop these scales and take a look

There's forty acres and redemption to be
found
Just along down the way
There is a place where no plow blade has
turned the ground
And you will turn it over, 'cause out here
hope remains
'Cause out here hope remains . . .

Out here the Texas sky is as big as the sea
And you're alone in your room like an
island floating free
Your spirit's hanging in a bottle out on a
tree
You say that you're the black sheep, I say
you're still family
So throw that bottle to the waves
They'll bring you in to me and from the
shore you will see

Out here the Texas rain is the hardest I've
ever seen
It'll wash your house away, but it'll also
make you clean
Now these rocks they are crying too
And this whole land is calling out for you

Action Steps

In "40 Acres," Caedmon's Call sings of the opportunity that each person has to experience the incredible, unsurpassed grace of Jesus Christ. If you have never received his forgiveness for your past sins and failures, then consider the following steps:

Get alone with God and pray for forgiveness. Realize that no amount of sin, shame, and guilt in your life can keep you from the love of Jesus Christ. Simply come to him and he will cleanse you with his grace.

Take a prayer walk outside. Imagine yourself walking toward God's land of opportunity as "40 Acres" describes. Accept God's grace as you surrender your life to Christ.

When you experience hard times, specifically pray that Christ would use these difficulties to mold you into being more like him.

In quiet time with God, study John 8, paying particular attention to verses 34–37.

6

A Rembrandt in Disguise

For over three hundred years, a portrait of a Russian aristocrat hung in the homes of its many various owners. Some bought it for a modest price. Others received it as another piece of art in an inheritance. The painting itself seemed rather unremarkable: the likeness of a flamboyantly clothed nobleman, all decked out with a tall hat, long hair, and wavy moustache. It survived the trash heap over the centuries because of its age, not its artistic qualities.

During a routine cleaning, however, a recent owner began to grow curious of the peculiar way in which the work was painted. Inconsistencies in the strokes and texture could be seen. Much of the painting looked like it was slopped on by an amateur. But the brushwork under the man's nose was different: it had the look of a master artist's work. Convinced that there was more to this Russian aristocrat than met the eye, the owner sought expert help. Art experts examined the portrait closely and performed a series of tests. They eventually confirmed his suspicion—the piece was anything but the work of an unknown amateur. Underneath the gaudy hat, hair, and moustache was a true masterpiece: a self-portrait by Rembrandt, one of the greatest artists of all time.

The fantastic true-life story of the Rembrandt self-portrait serves as a vivid reminder that what we see with our eyes is not always the real picture. Sometimes what lies under the surface is what's genuine. This same truth applies to the Christian life: underneath the sin coating of

Underneath the sin coating of every individual is a person created in the perfect image of God.

every individual is a person created in the perfect image of God. In "Anyway," Nichole Nordeman uses the imagery of restoring a painting to explore how we can discover our true identity in Christ.

Overpainted Sin

Every human baby arriving in this world comes wrapped in sin. Our tendency to disobey, what Christians often call a *sin nature*, is a direct result of the disobedience of Adam and Eve long ago. Ever since that time, sin has been passed down from generation to generation. We don't have to ask for it; we just get it. Quite innocent and invisible for the first years, this sin starts to coat every square inch of our lives as we get older. As it does, layers and layers of dirt and dust build up to disguise the original "you" that lies underneath.

As Nordeman begins "Anyway," she sings about the realization that "something must be underneath" all of the "dirty, dusty" sin in her life:

> Bless the day
> This restoration is complete
> Dirty dusty something must be underneath

When we become aware of our sin and ask Jesus to be our Savior, we start to realize that something about us is different—that we are more than just an empty shell of pride and disobedience. Yet, as new believers, we can struggle to understand exactly who is underneath.

Art restorers face the same problem with an overpainted picture. At first the original paint and the overpaint—the coating added on top of the dried original coat—look indistinguishable from each other. However, as the painting ages, the overpaint will gradually start to darken, while the original coat retains its color. As time passes, determining what paint is original and what coats were applied later becomes easier. Similarly, when we first become a Christian, our sin is still so tightly part of us that we have a very difficult time separating our sin nature from who we are. However, as we mature in our faith, layers of sin start to become more and more obvious. Behavior that we never gave a second thought to suddenly becomes convicting.

The more we become aware of these countless layers of sin, the more humble and sober we feel about ourselves. "I am the worst of all sinners," said the apostle Paul (see 1 Tim. 1:15), expressing what most sincere believers have felt at one time or another in their lives. Nordeman reflects this attitude in the second verse when she sings, "A gallery of paintings new and paintings old / I guess it's no surprise that I'm no Michelangelo." Michelangelo was arguably the greatest of all artists. And just as any overpainted picture is inferior to a Michelangelo, so too you and I are nothing compared to God's standard for holiness, Jesus Christ.

However, Nordeman doesn't stop here and wallow in self-pity. Instead, she delivers a great promise in the next line: "Every layer of mine hides a lovely design." In other words, she reminds us that while you and I aren't a perfect Michelangelo, we aren't just a sloppy Russian nobleman either. No, underneath the dusty, dirty sin in our lives is a person who was perfectly created in God's image. Only the sin coating disguises the beauty Christ intended for all people. Your original design, the real "you," is priceless and beautiful.

Scraping and Scuffing

Art restorers call overpainted works *composite figures*. That term is an appropriate description for Christians as well—we are each a mixture of ugly sin and "lovely design." And just as an art restorer works to remove the overpaint from the original, so too the Christian life involves removing the sin from our lives to expose God's perfect design. This work, however, is hard, as Nordeman alludes to when she sings:

> So I scrape and I scuff
> Though it's never quite enough
> I'm starting to see me finally

When art experts worked to restore the self-portrait of Rembrandt, the process was painstaking. Layers of paint had to be scraped away to reveal the original work. They could use solvents to remove the easy stuff. But in order to remove all of the overpaint without damaging the original, they had to use a tool called a micro-scalpel. In all, the restorers took six long years to complete the job. In the same way, the process of removing sin in our lives and becoming more Christlike is exacting and difficult. We have to "scrape and scuff" off our sin nature to let our true selves show through. In Nordeman's words, "It might take a little patience / it might take a little time." Yet as we surrender to Christ in the process, we will one day be able to say, "I'm starting to see me finally."

However, while Nordeman talks about our part in the restoration process, we must keep in mind who started it all off:

> You who have begun this work will someday see
> A portrait of the holiness you meant for me
> So I polish and shine
> Till it's easier to find even an outline of mine

Philosopher Søren Kierkegaard once said, "And now, with God's help, I shall become myself." We are to "scrape and scrub" and "polish and shine" but also remember that Christ is the one who begins this work and will complete it (Phil. 1:6). We need his help to become the person he intended us to be.

C. S. Lewis captures the essence of Christ's role in the removal of our sin in *The Voyage of the* Dawn Treader, part of his Chronicles of Narnia. In the story, a boy named Eustace goes to the world of Narnia kicking and screaming. An immature twit, he whines, insults, and drives others around him crazy. One day an act of recklessness causes him to be magically turned into a dragon. As a fire-breathing monster, he slowly begins to realize how terrible he had always been as a boy.

One night the Christ-figure lion named Aslan comes to the aid of Eustace the dragon. Aslan tells him to enter a pool of water but says that he has to shed his dragon skin first. As Eustace begins to scratch all over his body, nasty-looking scales start to fall off all around him. Thinking he has the skin removed, he starts to enter the pool. But as he does so, Eustace notices that his foot still looks much like it did before. So he scratches and peels another layer, and then a third layer. He eventually grows discouraged and wonders how many layers of skin he has to rip off. Finally, Aslan says to him, "You will have to let *me* undress you."[1] Eustace is scared of Aslan's claws, but he is so desperate that he lets Aslan do it anyway. The first rips are so deep and painful that Eustace is certain the claws have gone straight into his heart. But Eustace recalls later,

> He peeled the beastly stuff right off—just as I thought I'd done it myself the other three times . . . and there it was lying on the grass: only ever so much thicker, and darker, and more knobbly looking

The Christian life involves removing the sin from our lives to expose God's perfect design.

than the others had been. . . .Then he caught hold of me . . . and threw me into the water. It smarted like anything but only for a moment. After that it became perfectly delicious and as soon as I started swimming and splashing I found that all the pain had gone from my arm. And then I saw why. I'd turned into a boy again.[2]

In this story, Eustace was able to shed some of the layers of dragon skin by himself, but not all of them. He needed Aslan to truly cleanse and restore him. In the same way, by sheer will-power, we can conquer some sins with "polish and shine." Not the nasty, deep-seated ones, however. Only when we surrender these areas of our lives to Christ will he conquer those layers that we cannot rip off on our own. But when this happens, we will begin to see more and more of the "portrait of the holiness" that Nordeman sings about.

How God Sees You

For hundreds of years, the many owners of the priceless Rembrandt failed to realize the value of the artwork they had on their wall. They accepted the painting at face value. Likewise, when we look in the mirror and only see sin, we can feel pretty worthless. But that image is not how God sees us. The wonderful news of Christianity is that when we confess our sins and turn away from them, God sees us white as snow. Incredibly, we are considered pure and holy in his sight. Nordeman sings about this amazing truth in the chorus of "Anyway":

> But you called me beautiful
> When you saw my shame
> And you placed me on the wall
> Anyway

Because of the blood that Christ shed on the cross for us, God *already* calls us "beautiful." This promise is not something for the future—that you will be called worthy when you have finally removed all the sin from your life. No, the Bible says that if you are born again (John 3:3), the Lord calls you "beautiful" *today*.

What's more, Nordeman says, in spite of our guilt and shame, God places our picture on the wall. What an incredible image of God's enthusiastic love for you! He is so thrilled about who you are that he just has to have your portrait hanging up for all in heaven to see.

As the art restorers labored to return the Rembrandt self-portrait to its original glory, they were confident of its authenticity. But one final discovery eliminated all doubt. As they scraped the overpaint from a bottom corner, they were overjoyed to find Rembrandt's signature and a date of 1634 brushed on the original. In the same way, when the layers of sin are one day finally scraped away, we will discover God's signature clearly inscribed. That's the final bit of evidence of a true masterpiece. It's just waiting to be discovered inside of us.

ANYWAY
by Nichole Nordeman

Bless the day
This restoration is complete
Dirty dusty something must be underneath
So I scrape and I scuff
Though it's never quite enough
I'm starting to see me finally

A gallery of paintings new and paintings
  old
I guess it's no surprise that I'm no
  Michelangelo
Every layer of mine hides a lovely design
It might take a little patience
It might take a little time

But you called me beautiful
When you saw my shame
And you placed me on the wall
Anyway

You who have begun this work will
  someday see
A portrait of the holiness you meant for me
So I polish and shine
Till it's easier to find even an outline of
  mine

But you called me beautiful
When you saw my shame
And you placed me on the wall
Anyway
Anyway
And you placed me on the wall
Anyway

★★★ diving deeper ★★★

Read Psalms 14:1-3; 51:5; Jeremiah 17:9; Romans 3:23.

A Rembrandt in Disguise

Action Steps

In "Anyway," Nichole Nordeman explores who she really is behind the sin that covers her up. As you think about your own walk with Christ, pray about the following steps:

- On a piece of paper, write down the coats of sin you see painted on in your life. Confess each of them to God, and as you do, rip up the paper. Recognize that you can't remove all of your sin by sheer willpower. Jesus Christ is the one who both gives you the power to overcome your sin when you surrender your life to him and equips you with a scalpel and a scrubber.

- In a time of prayer, thank God for his grace. Remember that you don't have to be any more perfect in order for God to accept you. God already looks through your coats of sin to see you as a beautiful masterpiece today.

- Be realistic when you get frustrated with yourself. Restoring a masterpiece is a long-term process. In the same way, the restoration of your true self is a process that begins the moment you become a Christian and doesn't finish until you go to be with Christ in eternity. Yet God promises that one day this restoration process will be complete.

(More Than)
Creatures
for a
While

The Darwin fish. You have probably seen this emblem on the back of cars as you've driven down the highway. This symbol boldly proclaims that nature is all there is and all there ever will be. It is also a not-so-subtle jab at the Christian fish, or *Ichthus* symbol. Symbolizing the gospel, the Ichthus broadcasts a far different message: that *Jesus* is all there is and ever will be.

The Darwin fish and the Ichthus serve as symbols for the two dominant worldviews of this digital age. Each offers radically different answers as to how life came to be and what it means. On one hand, Darwinism speaks of human life evolving in a "survival of the fittest" manner. We see this worldview everywhere; schoolbooks, university courses, and the media talk about evolution as a given, a no-brainer. Listen to secular radio and you will discover that Darwinism creeps into popular music as well. Darwin lurks underneath every song that rants about a meaningless life or raves about the pursuit of fun at all costs.

We are far more than just creatures existing for a while.

Christianity, on the other hand, offers a much different take on things. As Audio Adrenaline sings about in "Original Species," we are far more than just creatures existing for a while. Instead, we each have eternal worth as a unique person made in the likeness of a personal and loving God.

Supernatural Selection

Most everyone has heard the name Charles Darwin, whether as a biochemist or a student struggling through high school biology class. Darwin, who lived back in the 1800s, is famous for popularizing the theory of evolution, the idea that all of life evolved through a process called "natural selection." While his theories were radical when he published his book *The Origin of Species*, they eventually became mainstream as philosophies like naturalism gained popularity and society became more and more secularized.

Not only did Darwin change the way people looked at the world and its origins, but his theory also changed the way people looked at themselves. In Darwin's world, humans were not uniquely created individuals. Instead, they were nothing more than animals that evolved through a random process. As a result, human life no longer had any meaning or purpose in and of itself; the new reality was that each person was born by accident, had a pulse for a few dozen years, and would someday keel over and turn back into dirt once again.

In contrast to Darwin's view of the world, Audio Adrenaline launches into "Original Species" by offering the Christian perspective of life:

Now my heart and mind agree
A super natural selected me
I see a plan so grandiose
My very own Galapagos

While Darwin popularized the theory of natural selection, Audio Adrenaline says that, in reality, there is a far different process at work: *supernatural selection*. God not only created the world but also was involved in the intricate details of how you personally came to be. In fact, he knew and selected you before you were even born. This idea that "a super natural selected me" is not just a clever lyric but exactly what the Bible speaks of in Jeremiah 1:5: "Before I formed you in the womb I knew you, before you were born I set you apart."

Darwin's inspiration for his evolutionary theories came from a trip he made to the Galapagos Islands in the Pacific Ocean. Audio Adrenaline's "own Galapagos" is found within the first chapter of Genesis, the spot in the Bible where God lays out his plan for humans. The remainder of the first verse of "Original Species" describes what this design was:

God laid down and he began to trace
An image that He could embrace
Then He smiled down on His plan
And from the dust He made a man

As Audio Adrenaline puts it, God "began to trace an image" of himself. He created people in his own likeness, giving them the ability to think, make decisions, feel emotions, and live forever. And when God was finished with the design, he was thrilled. Or in the words of Audio Adrenaline, "He smiled down on his plan."

Because God knows everything—past, present, and future—his plan for humans from the beginning actually had two parts: creation and redemption. Perhaps this is what Audio Adrenaline is getting at when they sing a lyric that can be taken two ways: "God laid down and began to trace / An image that He could embrace." You have already seen one meaning of how God "laid down," figuratively speaking—to make humans in his likeness. Yet the line has a second meaning, one that hints at Jesus Christ himself. God's relationship with man was severed because of Adam and Eve's sin. As a result, to restore the relationship, God had to come to earth himself as a man, Jesus Christ, and die for the sins of the world. In this way, Jesus "laid down" his life on the cross so that God could "embrace" humans once again.

More Than Enlightened

While Darwin advanced the idea of a world without God on the scientific front, Friedrich Nietzsche carried this torch into the field of philosophy at the end of the nineteenth century. Nietzsche is famous for proclaiming to the world that "God is dead, and we have killed him." To Nietzsche, because God is not around, life is ridiculous: people exist and then they die, with nothing that really matters happening in between.

As "Original Species" continues, Audio Adrenaline contrasts Nietzsche's so-called "enlightened" view of life with a far more optimistic view straight from the pages of the Bible:

I'm an original species
More enlightened than Nietzsche
I'm sure you'd like to meet me
I am loved
By the maker who's so clever
I was made to live forever
Though my body turns to sand
My soul is in His hands

Audio Adrenaline here highlights three fundamental differences between the way a Christian looks at himself and how Nietzsche or Darwin would.

First, no matter who you are, you are a person of worth. In Darwin's world, since the strongest and fittest are the survivors, successful people are naturally worth more than the losers of society; our value is based on what we *do* rather than who we *are.* Ultimately, our status, our achievements, or the amount of cash in our wallets is all that matters. In "Original Species," Audio Adrenaline offers a far different picture of the worth of each person. When they sing, "I'm sure you'd like to meet me," they are not bragging about any fame they may have gained as a popular Christian band. Instead, they are simply stating a basic truth of Christianity—that each living person is worth so much that they are sought after by God.

In our celebrity-obsessed culture, people go nuts at the chance to meet a well-known personality. Have you ever met a star actor or athlete at an autograph session or through an accidental encounter at an airport? If so, you were not only thrilled at the time but probably relived that moment with others in the years that followed. But we do not behave that way toward everyone we meet. We may go crazy trying to meet Audio Adrenaline while blowing off a homeless man in our rush to meet the band. But we will not always have this double standard; someday we will understand the worth of a person as God does today. In fact, our thrill at meeting the lowest and poorest of Christians in heaven will be far greater than would be the excitement of meeting your favorite band today.

Second, you are loved by the God who made you. Each person is not only selected by God before they are born but loved by him too. Audio Adrenaline sings, "I am loved by the maker who's so clever." The reality of God's love sweeps through the pages of the Bible, from his plan of creation to the sacrificial death of Jesus to the heaven he's got in store for believers in the future. In contrast, in Darwin and Nietzsche's world, not only is life pointless, but love

Each living person is worth so much that they are sought after by God.

and emotion are purely the results of electrical charges running through the brain.

Third, you are designed to live forever. From a Darwinist view, the biological wheels that are set in motion at your birth gradually slow down over your lifetime, someday grinding to a halt. Since the physical world is all there is, the idea that you have a soul that lives on is flatly rejected. In "Original Species," Audio Adrenaline begs to differ. Your wheels, once set in motion from day one, will never stop. You are an "original species," uniquely handcrafted by God for eternity. Your earthly "body turns to sand" when you die, but your soul is "made to live forever."

Facts of Faith

When we look at how these two worldviews stand up to the facts, the popular opinion is that the bulk of evidence is all in Darwin's court. Evolution is described as "scientific fact" while creation by God is dismissed as a "religious fairy tale." Once again, Audio Adrenaline disagrees. The band starts out "Original Species" by emphasizing that Christianity combines faith and fact. When they sing, "Now my heart and mind agree," they speak of facts working hand in hand with Christianity's claims of truth. As a result, Christians never need to be worried about discoveries in the worlds of science or archaeology. We can have confidence that when all of the evidence is discovered, it will always support Christian faith. Or, as author Win Corduan says, "I am convinced that faith and reason, if used properly, will arrive at identical truth."[1]

One of the ways we can see proof of God's involvement in creation is simply looking at the world around us. The complexity and diversity of the universe scream out for a designer behind it all. In the last verse Audio Adrenaline speaks of this "breakthrough theory of origin," which is actually the "simple truth" that has been found in the Bible all along:

A breakthrough theory of origin
A simple truth that's always been
Fingerprints have been left behind
That point us to a master mind
Stars in the sky
There to please my eye

If we are sincerely honest in our search for God in creation, says Audio Adrenaline, we will find him. Jeremiah 29:13 also promises that we will find God when we seek him with all of our hearts and minds. Countless examples from nature can point us to God as a designer—the majesty of the mountains, the stars in the night sky, the miracle of a human birth, and the complexities of the cell. Each of these "fingerprints" can "point us to a master mind," the one God who designed and created it all. The choice every person has in life is whether to look honestly for those fingerprints or dismiss them as cosmic accidents.

The Infinite, Up Close

In "Original Species," Audio Adrenaline focuses on the issue of origins, or how the world was created. But underneath the surface, the band is also singing about far more personal and significant issues—who we are and why we are here. Exactly how we answer those questions depends on our worldview. If you choose to live life with a Darwin fish logo on your bumper, then life is pointless, meaningless, and without hope. In fact, your only way out of total despair is to ignore what you say you believe and cling to some meaning and purpose anyway, wherever you can find it.

However, Audio Adrenaline offers an alternative. In the final lines of "Original Species," the band sings that the God who has "the cosmos in His command" also has "time to hold my hand." In other words, the very same God who is powerful enough to create the universe also desires a personal relationship with us. That's the incredible truth and wonderful promise of Christianity, for within God's plan, he gives us all the freedom, meaning, love, and worth that we could ever wish for.

Survival of the fittest? That's so nineteenth century. Instead, the one answer to the origins of life that will never go out of fashion can be summed up by a much more hopeful catchphrase—the *thriving of the loved.*

ORIGINAL SPECIES
by Audio Adrenaline

Now my heart and mind agree
A super natural selected me
I see a plan so grandiose
My very own Galapagos
God laid down and he began to trace
An image that He could embrace
Then He smiled down on His plan
And from the dust He made a man

I'm an original species
More enlightened than Nietzsche
I'm sure you'd like to meet me
I am loved
By the maker who's so clever
I was made to live forever
Though my body turns to sand
My soul is in His hands

A breakthrough theory of origin
A simple truth that's always been
Fingerprints have been left behind
That point us to a master mind
Stars in the sky
There to please my eye
The cosmos in His command
But He has time to hold my hand

Action Steps

In "Original Species," Audio Adrenaline sings about the origins of life and how that relates to who we are and our place in this universe. The song says that you didn't come about because of an evolutionary process but were created by a loving, personal God in his image. As you consider this, apply the following action steps to your Christian walk:

- When you watch movies or listen to songs, recognize the worldview that is being communicated. Realize the influence that a Darwinian worldview can have on you without you even knowing it.

- Talk to your non-Christian friends about their beliefs about the origins of life. Discuss the kind of purposeless life we would be left with in a world without God.

- If you struggle with your self-image, read the Bible with an eye on what it says about you—that you are a person of infinite worth. Cling to the promises that you were selected by God before you were even born and were raised up for such a time as this (Jer. 1:5; 29:11).

- If you struggle with doubts about the truth of the Christian view on creation, don't run away from them. First, be honest with God about your struggle and ask him to lead you as you work through the doubts. Second, research the questions you have, looking at the evidence for Darwinism and Christianity.

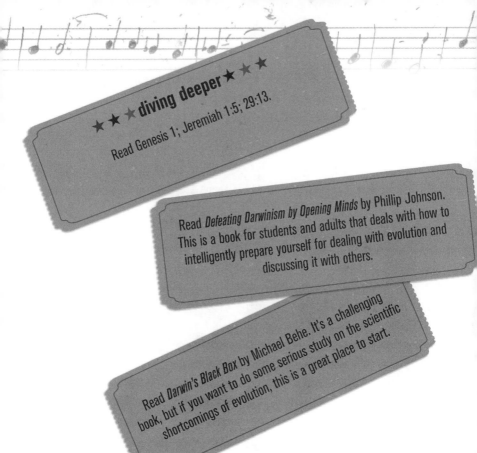

★ ★ ★ **diving deeper** ★ ★ ★

Read Genesis 1; Jeremiah 1:5; 29:13.

Read *Defeating Darwinism by Opening Minds* by Phillip Johnson. This is a book for students and adults that deals with how to intelligently prepare yourself for dealing with evolution and discussing it with others.

Read *Darwin's Black Box* by Michael Behe. It's a challenging book, but if you want to do some serious study on the scientific shortcomings of evolution, this is a great place to start.

Part Three

Life and Mea

When wings beat the night sky 'bove the ground
Will I unwillingly shoot them down
With all my petty fears and doubts, down, down?
  Sixpence None the Richer, "We Have Forgotten"

We're waiting for the day
We'll hear the Father say
Yeah, to hear him say
"Well done, good and faithful one
Enter in, come on, share with me
Welcome home, good and faithful one
On and on through eternity . . ."
           Newsboys, "Hallelujah"

8

True
Greatness

We see slogans like Be like Mike or Live like Lance popping up all the time in television commercials. These ad campaigns are designed to appeal to a deep need inside of us—the desire to be great. If you drink the sports drink of a basketball legend or eat the energy bar of a Tour de France champ, then you too can be a winner. Companies use these techniques because they work: champions sell products because we want to be like them.

Celebrity endorsements are just the tip of the iceberg for how our pop culture worships greatness. The fashion industry knows we make buying decisions based on what the hottest music star wears onstage or the all-star NBA player wears on his feet. This obsession with heroes often goes beyond our clothes closets and eats into our calendars as well. Some people are so captivated by stars, they just can't get enough. They absorb the latest gossip on *E!*, faithfully scour *People*, join fan clubs, and spend hours chatting on fan websites.

When we read some of the stories in the Old Testament about people bowing down and worshiping golden idols, we may roll our eyes. After all, who today would actually kneel before a golden calf and worship it? Yet when we look at how our world treats celebrities, the similarities are actually quite shocking. Oh, you probably don't bow down before an autographed picture of Tom Cruise. But you can idolize him in different, more sophisticated ways. If you do, the result is the same: hero worship. Even the names we give to celebrities reveal what we really think of them: they are *idols*, *megastars*, and sometimes even *gods*.

As Christians we may shake our heads at the idol worship of pop culture. But watch out—the Christian community can slip into this same trap. Go to a concert of any major Contemporary

Christian Music band. You won't see the drugs you might see at a secular gathering, but you'll still see thousands of crazed fans who revere the band as rock idols. Even popular Christian speakers and pastors can be placed on such high pedestals that they become the Christianized version of a megastar. Without even realizing it, we can even come to think of our Christian hero's words as being on the same level as the words of Jesus himself.

Even the names we give to celebrities reveal what we really think of them: they are idols, megastars, and sometimes even gods.

We are drawn to great people because greatness is something we crave for ourselves. Some of us are driven to copycat their success and emerge as the next big star. Or maybe we are content to simply look on at the triumphs of others and hope that some of that "pixie dust" sprinkles onto us. Either way, we want to rub shoulders with greatness. It makes us feel like we matter.

Ten Shekel Shirt explores this deep-seated need for greatness inside of every person in their song "Great." True greatness, sings the band, is not found by latching onto others or by striving for worldly success. Instead, it can only be attained by looking at the true meaning of significance through the eyes of Jesus Christ.

Some Christians may complain that striving for greatness is nothing but an ego trip, the exact opposite of what a disciple should be concerned about. But as Ten Shekel Shirt points out, if our focus is on Christ, this longing does not need to be a self-centered obsession.

Great Expectations

Everybody wants to have something in their life that they can point to and say they are the best at it. Ten Shekel Shirt starts off "Great" by vocalizing this universal wish:

I have always wanted to be somebody who is great

As we grow up, the sky's the limit. Dreams of greatness dance through our heads as we imagine making it as a pro athlete, a movie star, or a renowned artist. But as we get older, we usually find ourselves unable to reach those lofty peaks. Unshaken, we gradually lower our expectations to something we can pull off—perhaps making the city all-star team, getting accepted into the right college, or rising faster than others on the corporate ladder. This instinctive desire for achievement and success is God-given. But the problem sets in when our aspirations spin out of control and we lose perspective. We can become consumed by an ego-driven charge to make a name for ourselves.

While the world applauds that kind of win-at-all-costs drive, Christianity does not. As believers, we are called to be set apart, to be different from what is normal. Therefore, the desire of a believer to "be someone" is not for personal glory but for God's glory. As Ten Shekel Shirt continues, they talk about this perspective, revealing the secret dream buried in the heart of every disciple:

To be great in, great in your eyes, is my dream
To be the one who makes you smile is everything

In attempting to live out this dream, a natural next step is a "go get 'em" approach—to redirect our energies away from worldly pursuits and to doing big things for God instead. We may decide to become the next Billy Graham or Rebecca St.

James, reaching millions for Christ. These are great goals, but watch out: even worthy dreams can be twisted by Satan into something bad. The danger lies when we become consumed with wanting to "make a difference." We can start to do God's work not for Christ's sake but for our own sake. We can put a Christian wrapper around a raw quest for greatness.

I experienced that distraction a few years ago. *Christianity Today* magazine had a cover story featuring thirty up-and-coming young Christian leaders, much like *People* might showcase fast-rising Hollywood stars. As I read the article, I immediately felt competitive. Here was a list of future Christian movers and shakers—and lo and behold, my name was not on that list! In my selfish pride, I became more concerned with making a name for myself in a ministry than with serving God with a pure and humble heart. Whenever we get sidetracked, our objectives can turn into self-centeredness, even as we are doing God's work.

Whether we are working in the secular world or in a Christian ministry, this desire for greatness is a dangerous beast. In the bridge of "Great," Ten Shekel Shirt brings a dose of reality back into the picture and gets to the heart of the matter:

> Greatness in this world is different than greatness in your eyes

Ten Shekel Shirt points out that significance is a whole different gig for God than it is for the world around us. Consider three differences in particular:

First, worldly greatness is self-centered, while true greatness forgets about self. Apart from God, the desire to be great will always turn into a "me" love fest; the holy trinity in our lives becomes "me, myself, and I." That's why there are so many "divas" on Hollywood sets and so few champion athletes or rock stars with genuine humility. This ego trip is exactly what led the disciples James and John to want to be a cut above the others, even prodding their mom to ask Jesus if they could sit next to him in his future kingdom (see Matt. 20:20–28). Amazingly, these two "diva disciples" did not even realize how outrageous such a request was in the eyes of their Lord. But in his loving way, Jesus reminded James and John that greatness in the eyes of the world is focused on self-centered power and influence, but in God's eyes, "whoever wants to become great among you must be your servant, and whoever wants to be first must be your slave" (Matt. 20:26–27). Jesus understood completely that as we serve others, we begin to dwell less and less on our own petty concerns and learn more and more how to bring glory to him.

Second, greatness in the world is based on accomplishments; greatness in God's eyes is based on the heart. To be great in the world's eyes, one must be successful. Silver medalists don't get the shoe contracts. Super Bowl losers miss out on the Disney World trips. Instead, legends are built on winning championships. To the world, winning is the only thing that matters. But greatness in God's eyes has nothing to do with success. In fact, success is not mentioned once in Scripture as an aim for the Christian disciple. As Oswald Chambers said, Jesus Christ never calls you to be successful; he calls you to be faithful.[1] Clearly, then, Christ is far less concerned about your victories for the gospel than he is about the state of your heart as you work for him. Truth be told, Jesus much prefers a lone obedient loser to a handful of ego-driven winners.

Third, the world's greatness is short-lived, while true greatness is eternal. Significance in the world is like a

To the world, winning is the only thing that matters. But greatness in God's eyes has nothing to do with success.

Lif and Meaning

shooting star—brilliant one moment but fading away the next. Nearly all the pop idols from a decade ago have long since left the scene. And only a handful of celebrities ever survive over the long haul. The fleeting nature of stardom is memorably revealed in the film *Notting Hill*. Julia Roberts plays Anna Scott, a major film star who, in a quiet moment, candidly reflects on her probable future:

> One day, not long from now, my looks will go. They will discover I can't act, and I will become some sad middle-aged woman who looks a bit like someone who was famous for a while.

Anna's description of fading glory is a dead-on description of worldly greatness. Whether it lasts for a year, a decade, or occasionally a lifetime, earthly significance always vanishes and wastes away in the end. Greatness in God's eyes, however, never fades. The treasures you store up in heaven as you please Jesus Christ will last forever.

Another Kind of Great

Since God's idea of greatness is radically different from the world's definition, how can a disciple become great without getting derailed by selfish pride? The song "Great" is, at its heart, an exploration of that issue. Ten Shekel Shirt highlights three key disciplines that we should make part of our Christian walk as we seek to be great.

Love your enemies. When Ten Shekel Shirt sings that to be great is to "love my enemies," they are pointing to something Jesus taught his followers in the Sermon on the Mount: "Love your enemies and pray for those who persecute you" (Matt. 5:44). Christ is not talking about being polite or biting your tongue. He wants you to go all out in serving and sacrificing for someone you cannot stand.

"To love a person," Fyodor Dostoevsky once said, "means to see him as God intended him to be."[2] In other words, you do not look at how your enemy is today but see how that person would be with Christ working in his or her life. Such a feat is only accomplished through God's grace working in your heart. When you hand over your hatred and bitterness to him, you can, to borrow the words of Christian author Philip Yancey, begin to look at your enemies with "grace-healed" eyes.

Serve others sacrificially. The second discipline Ten Shekel Shirt mentions is to "serve others until I become the least." Jesus gave his disciples a firsthand example of what it means to lower yourself before others by washing his disciples' feet (see John 13:1–17). True greatness empties out your ego as you do things that you could never take pride in or become smug about.

Love God and others. The final activity that Ten Shekel Shirt mentions is "to be genuine in my love for others and for you." After all, if we earnestly love God and others around us, everything else falls into place. Sometimes, however, genuinely loving someone else is easier said than done. Maybe our neighbor is a grouch, or maybe we just don't feel like loving another person. C. S. Lewis reminds us that we shouldn't focus on how we *feel* about loving someone else; instead, we should just *do* it. He wrote, "Do not waste time bothering whether you 'love' your neighbor; act as if you did. As soon as we do this we find one of the great secrets, When you are behaving as if you loved someone, you will . . . come to love him."[3]

As we make these three practices part of our lives, they completely transform our outlook. We stop obsessing over ourselves because we are busy living for God and trying to serve others. That's exactly Ten Shekel Shirt's point. When we throw out the ego trips, the greatness that we've been searching for all along floods into our lives. But, in a most unexpected surprise, the source of this greatness isn't us but Jesus himself. That's why, in the end, the real secret of achieving greatness is rather straightforward: *dim yourself and Christ will shine his greatness through you.*

In a world that longs to be like Mike, be like Christ. In a society that says you matter if you live like Lance, live like Jesus would. In the end, the celebrity television spots do get one thing right: we desire greatness. But they are wrong about the person we are really striving to become. We are searching not for the fleeting success of the Michael Jordans or Lance Armstrongs of the world but for the never-ending greatness of Jesus.

GREAT
bu Ten Shekel Shirt

I have always wanted to be somebody who is great

To be great in, great in your eyes, is my dream
To be the one who makes you smile is everything

To love my enemies
To serve others until I become the least

To be great in, great in your eyes, is my dream
To be the one who makes you smile is everything

Greatness in this world is different than greatness in your eyes

To be great in, great in your eyes, is my dream
To be the one who makes you smile is everything

To be genuine in my love for others and for you is to be great

Action Steps

In "Great," Ten Shekel Shirt contrasts greatness in the eyes of the world with what is great to God. As you strive for significance, take the following steps as part of your Christian walk:

- Write down a list of things that you can do in your life to achieve greatness in God's eyes, not in the eyes of the world.

- Avoid hero worship, especially among your favorite Christian music artists. Feel free to enjoy their success, but don't try to find meaning by living your life through them.

- In all you do, strive for obedience, not success. Simply do God's work and let him worry about the success or failure of your efforts.

- Above all, love your enemies, serve others sacrificially, and love God and your neighbor with a pure and humble heart. This week, go out of your way to serve your friend or neighbor as an expression of love.

★ ★ ★ diving deeper ★ ★ ★

Read Matthew 5; 20:20-28; John 13:14-17.

Meaning

More

I urge you to live a life worthy of the calling you have received.

Ephesians 4:1

In the film *Field of Dreams*, Ray Kinsella is a farmer who hears a mysterious voice in his cornfield speaking what has become one of the most quoted lines in movie history: "*If you build it, he will come.*" Ray is faced with the dilemma of whether or not to follow the voice and plow up his corn to build a baseball field. If he does, he will put his family's finances in jeopardy. But if he ignores it, Ray is convinced he will turn into someone just like his father, a person who gave up on his dreams. Debating his decision, Ray reflects on his father:

> He must have had dreams, but he never did anything about them. For all I know, he may have even heard voices too, but he sure didn't listen to them . . . I'm afraid of that happening to me. And something is telling me this might be the last chance I have to do something about it. I want to build that field.

When faced with the choice of whether to live out their dreams, Ray and his father took radically different paths. His dad, perhaps stung by past failure or the pressure to be normal, settled for an ordinary life. Ray chose another, far more uncertain path.

During the course of our Christian lives, we're going to be confronted with a similar dilemma. No, you probably aren't going to hear an actual voice in a cornfield. But you are going to have a choice: pursue a dream, a calling from God, that may look risky from a human point of view, or else opt for a more sensible way of life. Yet even when we are convinced of what

God has called us to do and decide to do it, making it happen is never easy. In fact, the pursuit of a dream can leave us searching for answers, particularly when we encounter failure and disillusionment along the way.

Sixpence None the Richer and Switchfoot have each written songs that deal with the struggles Christians face trying to experience all that God has for them. Sixpence's "We Have Forgotten" centers on the tragedy of letting our shattered dreams drag us down. Switchfoot's "Meant to Live" serves as a wake-up call, reminding believers that we are made for so much more than a life of forgotten plans.

Crash and Burn

As "We Have Forgotten" begins, Sixpence perfectly captures the otherworldly quality of dreams, calling them "inconsistent angel things." In other words, they're real but hard to explain; they're from heaven but wildly unpredictable played out on earth. And much like "horses bred with star-laced wings," dreams are beautiful, full of promise, and yet often unrealistic to someone on the outside looking in.

Christians and non-Christians alike have dreams, but to the believer a dream carries special significance: it can serve as one's calling in life. Its fulfillment can be seen as living out Jesus's promise of John 10:10, "I have come that they may have life, and that they may have it more abundantly" (NKJV). Dreams can take many shapes and forms, such as getting into the right college, being hired at that fast-rising start-up, making the Olympic team, marrying your dream girl, or becoming a missionary. A God-

Yet even when we are convinced of what God has called us to do and decide to do it, making it happen is never easy.

inspired vision gives us purpose in life, a feeling of significance, and a reason for getting out of bed each day. And the pursuit of that goal can become one of the primary ways in which we express our faith in Christ.

But dreams, at least those really worth having, are not easily attained. It's hard to make them fly. And more often than not, we can find them crashing and burning before our eyes. In the first verse of "We Have Forgotten," Sixpence talks about the fragile, uncertain nature of dreams and the sobering reality of them hitting the ground:

> Dreams, inconsistent angel things
> Horses bred with star-laced wings
> But it's hard to make them fly, fly, fly
> These wings beat the night sky 'bove the town
> One goes up and one goes down
> And so the chariot hits the ground, bound, bound

Little is more discouraging in a Christian's life than having a plan you believe to be from God go unfulfilled. Sometimes these dreams are shot down by an outside event. Perhaps the college rejects your application, the start-up company hires your best friend instead, or your fiancée is killed in a tragic accident. At other times, a dream can be bound up by something inside us. We may give up and leave it behind after encountering an obstacle, believing that we just aren't good enough or don't measure up.

When life isn't working out as we expected it to, these circumstances can send us into a tailspin. Our faith can be rocked as we wonder how God could possibly allow this to happen.

Or, even if we are willing to give God the benefit of the doubt, we may blame it all on ourselves and question our ability to know God's will and leading. At the start of "Meant to Live," Switchfoot expresses this uncertainty:

> Fumbling his confidence
> And wondering why the world has passed him by
> Hoping that he's bent for more than arguments
> And failed attempts to fly, fly

With our confidence shaken—whether in God or in ourselves—we naturally begin to compare our situation to those of others around us. We see a friend living out his dream while, as Switchfoot says, we wonder why the world has passed us by. Somehow, someway, we've gotten the short end of the stick; our attempts to fly have failed and left us battered and bruised. Dealing with that harsh reality can be hard to stomach and can leave us feeling abandoned and all alone.

Stockholm Syndrome

"Stockholm syndrome" is a phenomenon in which a person who is taken hostage during a robbery or terrorist act begins to identify and connect with the criminal. In fact, sometimes the hostage suffering from Stockholm syndrome bonds with the hostage taker to such a degree that he or she resists being rescued. That condition may seem puzzling to us, but in a very real way, that's exactly what can happen to us when we become disillusioned with life because of an unfulfilled dream. To survive the disappointment, we can begin to find security and comfort in our fallen surroundings, developing a "Stockholm syndrome" response to our failures.

The chorus of Sixpence's "We Have Forgotten" speaks to this phenomenon exactly. We can get into such a rut that we forget how it felt when our lives seemed to have meaning and purpose. Or, as the chorus goes:

> We have forgotten (Don't try to make me fly)
> How it used to be (I'll stay here, I'll be fine)
> How it used to be (Don't go and let me down)
> How it used to be (I'm starting to like this town)

Life becomes a shoulder shrug. We avoid investing emotionally in our dreams and desires. We settle. Not only do we stop making an effort to come out of the rut, but we actually become content in it. We start to "like this town" because living in this concrete jungle isolates us from further disappointment or testing by God. Or, to paraphrase C. S. Lewis, we become like a kid who wants to go on making mud pies in a slum because he cannot imagine what is meant by the offer of a trip to the beach.

When believers forget their dreams and the call of Christ to live as disciples, they quickly become absorbed into the world around them. Modern culture is relentless in its efforts to run us through a cookie cutter, to make us just like everyone else. One side of society, most often the youth culture, preaches the "be yourself gospel": rebel against convention, stand up for a cause (whatever it is), but don't force your beliefs on others. The other side, usually the older generations, pro- claims the "gospel

Life and Meaning

of common sense": go corporate, pursue stability, and play it smart. But neither of these so-called "gospels" is compatible with pursuing God's calling for our lives. That's why the Christian who chooses to live out the call to be "in the world but not of the world" faces a hard road; he's the one type of nonconformist who usually isn't smiled upon by either side. But when we feel God has let us down, we'll lose heart for walking that difficult path in between. The desire to live just like everyone else gives us a kind of Stockholm syndrome—the feeling that maybe the world isn't such a bad place to live in after all.

In addition to the pressure from the world around us, one of the traps that can prevent us from living out our God-sent dreams is sabotage. First, fear and doubt can actually lead us to shoot down our own dreams. The second verse of "We Have Forgotten" puts it like this:

When wings beat the night sky 'bove the ground
Will I unwillingly shoot them down
With all my petty fears and doubts, down, down!?

Experiencing failure can make us gun-shy of putting ourselves at risk again. We fear failure and doubt God's ability to change matters. So, in our minds, shooting down the dream ourselves becomes easier than risking the disappointment of being rejected by someone else.

Second, when we become disillusioned with living a life of faith, we can also start to sabotage the dreams of others. In the second chorus of the song, Sixpence sings about this selfish response:

> We have forgotten (Am I in love with this?)
> How it used to be (My constant broken ship)
> How it used to be (Don't go, I'll shoot you
> down)
> How it used to be (I'm starting to like this
> town)

As the old saying goes, misery loves company. When we allow disappointment to produce jealousy and bitterness inside our hearts, we will—consciously or unconsciously—shoot down the dreams of others around us. After all, if we aren't happy, why should anyone else be?

But when we allow sabotage—either of our own dreams or of the dreams of others—to enter our hearts, we need to take stock and realize just how far away we've moved from the apostle Paul's command in Ephesians 4:1: "I urge you to live a life worthy of the calling you have received." We've traded in the fruit of the Spirit—love, joy, peace, patience, kindness, goodness, faithfulness, gentleness, and self-control (Gal. 5:22–23)—for a spirit of fear, doubt, and bitterness.

More Life

In "We Have Forgotten," Sixpence shows the tragedy of living a life of broken dreams and the way in which it can sabotage our faith and the faith of others around us. In "Meant to Live," Switchfoot sounds the alarm bell and begins to push toward a way out of this problem. In the chorus Switchfoot seeks to wake us up from any effects of "Stockholm syndrome" that we may be suffering:

> We were meant to live for so much more
> Have we lost ourselves?

Somewhere we live inside
Somewhere we live inside
We were meant to live for so much more
Have we lost ourselves?
Somewhere we live inside

In the words of Sixpence, we may "have forgotten" and settled for what the world has to offer. But Switchfoot reminds us that we are "meant to live for so much more." We aren't meant to inhabit a world of comfort, common sense, and compromise. Instead, real life is "somewhere inside"; real life is living a life worthy of the calling we have received, one of risky adventure and uncertain outcome. That adventure may very well include dreams that crash and burn. But if we look through the flames, we'll always see God.

Second, after we've awakened from our spiritual daze, the next step is to simply try again. In the second verse of "Meant to Live," Switchfoot reflects on taking second chances:

Dreaming about Providence
And whether mice and men have second tries
Maybe we've been livin' with our eyes half open
Maybe we're bent and broken, broken

When life has turned out far differently from what we expected, we can feel, as Switchfoot puts it, "bent and broken." But if we offer our hopes and dreams to God, he will straighten and repair us. He'll get us fixed up to try again. Remember, we have a God of "second tries." The whole reason Jesus Christ came to earth was as a second try, so to speak, for the human race because humans couldn't become holy on their own.

Our third and final step is to recognize that God uses both our dreams and our failures for his purposes. Switchfoot hints at this truth during the final line of the bridge:

> We want more than this world's got to offer
> We want more than this world's got to offer
> We want more than the wars of our fathers
> And everything inside screams for second life, yeah

The fact that "everything inside screams for second life" should remind us of what we are really made for: we are eternal creatures, designed and built from the ground up for eternity. That's why God gives us a calling in the first place: to undertake a life pursuit that has significance and purpose not just for sixty years but forever. But because we are made for eternity, God has other plans to accomplish in our lives beyond our dreams. We focus on *what we can do* with our lives, but God is even more concerned about *who we can become*. Quite apart from our plans and desires, God has his own dream for our lives—to perfect and mold us into persons who are like Christ.

Once we realize God has this objective for us, we begin to see why living out our calling is always going to be tough stuff. If our dreams were easy to attain, then the inner transformation that God desires would never be realized. If our dreams were handed to us on a silver platter, then we would simply end up being filled with pride and trusting in our own capabilities rather than trusting God. That's why he allows dreams to hit the ground: hard times and failure produce humility, character, and a stronger faith, which are Christlike qualities that will stay with us forever.

Therefore, if we are going to pursue our calling outwardly while allowing God to change us inwardly, just one key can make these two objectives work together: endurance. Endurance is talked about all throughout the New Testament. The apostle Peter says that if you face hardship when doing God's work and you endure that hardship, take heart, because God is pleased (see 1 Peter 2:20). The apostle Paul tells Timothy to "keep your head in all situations and endure hardship" (2 Tim. 4:5). The writer of Hebrews joins the chorus: "Endure hardship as discipline" (Heb. 12:7). In the end, endurance is what allows us to press on toward our goal as God refines us.

Trading Places

In perhaps the most memorable scene from the epic film *Braveheart*, Scottish hero William Wallace prepares his soldiers to battle an English army that is far better trained and equipped than they are. The Scottish soldiers are scared, and many are preparing to leave the battlefield before fighting begins. When asked if they will fight, one man responds, "Against that? No. We will run, and we will live." On hearing this response, Wallace challenges his countrymen:

> Aye, fight and you may die; run, and you'll live . . . at least awhile. And dying in your beds, many years from now, would you be willing to trade all the days from this day to that for one chance—just one chance—to come back here and tell our enemies that they may take away our lives, but they'll never take our freedom?[1]

The life-or-death decision that each Scottish soldier faced on the battlefield that day is much like the choice that every Christian has to make in their life: Will you risk everything for God? Or should you "run and live"? Running in real life from risk and potential disappointment is the safest route and may help you find acceptance by your peers and security in the world. But fast-forward your life to a day fifty years from now. Sitting in your rocker and looking back on your life, do you think you would trade a lifetime of comfort, common sense, and compromise for just one shot at living the adventurous dream God has called you to?

Sixpence and Switchfoot show us the two ways that we can respond to that challenge. "We Have Forgotten" describes what happens when we forget our dreams and settle for the ordinary. "Meant to Live" urges us to take that second try, to risk failure, but in doing so, live for so much more. How will you respond?

MEANT TO LIVE
by Switchfoot

Fumbling his confidence
And wondering why the world has passed
him by
Hoping that he's bent for more than
arguments
And failed attempts to fly, fly

[Chorus:]
We were meant to live for so much more
Have we lost ourselves?
Somewhere we live inside
Somewhere we live inside
We were meant to live for so much more
Have we lost ourselves?
Somewhere we live inside

Dreaming about Providence
And whether mice and men have second
tries
Maybe we've been livin' with our eyes half
open
Maybe we're bent and broken, broken

[Chorus]
We want more than this world's got to offer
We want more than this world's got to offer
We want more than the wars of our fathers
And everything inside screams for second
life, yeah

We were meant to live for so much more
Have we lost ourselves?
We were meant to live for so much more
Have we lost ourselves?
We were meant to live for so much more
Have we lost ourselves?
We were meant to live
We were meant to live

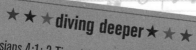

★ ★ ★ **diving deeper** ★ ★ ★

Read Ephesians 4:1; 2 Timothy 2:3; Hebrews 12:7; 1 Peter 2:20.
Read John Eldredge, *The Journey of Desire*.
Read Erwin McManus, *Seizing Your Divine Moment*.

WE HAVE FORGOTTEN
by Sixpence None the Richer

Dreams, inconsistent angel things
Horses bred with star-laced wings
But it's so hard to make them fly, fly, fly
These wings beat the night sky 'bove the town
One goes up and one goes down
And so the chariot hits the ground, bound, bound

We have forgotten (don't try to make me fly)
How it used to be (I'll stay here, I'll be fine)
How it used to be (don't go and let me down)
How it used to be (I'm starting to like this town)

When wings beat the night sky 'bove the ground
Will I unwillingly shoot them down
With all my petty fears and doubts, down, down?

We have forgotten (am I in love with this?)
How it used to be (my constant broken ship)
How it used to be (don't go, I'll shoot you down)
How it used to be (I'm starting to like this town)

Used by permission. [10]

Action Steps

Both Sixpence None the Richer's "We Have Forgotten" and Switchfoot's "Meant to Live" urge you to live out God's calling for your life and not settle for what the world has to offer. As you think about your life's dream, consider the following steps to help you start living it out:

Listen to Switchfoot's Beautiful Letdown album in one sitting. Prayerfully consider the many challenges concerning what's really important in your life that Switchfoot throws out at you throughout the CD. After you've listened to it, spend a few moments in prayer asking God for clear direction for your life.

Find your calling and pursue it with all your energy. Don't let expectations or common sense dictate God's call on your life. Discovering what exactly your calling is, however, can be one of life's greatest challenges. Kick off the process by fasting for 24 hours and praying during the time in which you would normally eat.

Talk with a Christian friend and challenge each other to live out all that Christ has called each of you to do.

10

Future
Glory

Eric Liddell and Pete Rose: two athletes participating in different sports and living in different eras. But each was legendary in his day for his grit and all-out determination to win. Eric Liddell was an Olympic gold medalist and one of the fastest men of the early twentieth century. Pete Rose was a baseball World Series winner in the 1970s and considered by many the greatest hitter of all time. Both Liddell and Rose were celebrated for their mental toughness, for being able to win on sheer willpower alone. On the surface, looking at their work ethics, attitudes, and accomplishments, they appear to be two athletes cut from the same cloth, separated only by decades and sports. However, when we start to look at what made each of them tick, we will see that the perspectives of the two sporting legends could hardly have been more different.

Pete Rose desperately wants to be remembered as one of the greatest baseball players of all time. But because of gambling trouble that he got himself into years ago, he is not eligible for the baseball hall of fame. Ever since his suspension, Rose has been consumed with getting his ban from baseball reversed. To Rose, his legacy—everything he wants to be known for—is directly linked to being voted into that exclusive club of baseball greats.

A disciple's "moment in the sun" isn't here on earth.

In stark contrast, Eric Liddell would have rolled his eyes at talk of any such awards for him. In fact, he would probably offer a shoulder shrug and then quickly change the subject to his real passion: spreading the gospel in China. The world's

Life and Meaning

recognition for his achievements meant nothing to him. Eric understood that for Christian disciples, what we achieve on the athletic field, in the classroom, or in the office does not define who we are. Instead, our calling is to press on toward things that matter for eternity rather than looking backwards at past accomplishments.

Nichole Nordeman and the Newsboys each perform songs that underscore the truth that a disciple's "moment in the sun" isn't here on earth. Instead, it comes only after we go to our Lord in heaven. In her song "Legacy," Nordeman sings about creating a legacy in heaven by doing things on this earth that really matter. The Newsboys' song "Hallelujah" continues this same theme as it explores the future glory that awaits us when we have served Christ on earth. And despite the hard times and suffering that we may encounter along the way, both Nordeman and the Newsboys encourage us to hold fast, because this future glory to come is worth the hard work and long wait.

Pictures, Busts, and Blurbs

In "Legacy," Nordeman sings about the tug-of-war that is waged in the heart of every disciple. We each have to decide, says Nordeman, whether we are living for "the temporary trappings of this world" or building the "kind of legacy" that really matters to Christ. Nordeman points out how enticing the attention of this world can be. She starts off "Legacy" singing, "I don't mind if you've got something nice to say about me / And I enjoy an accolade like the rest." Everyone is born with this desire to matter, to receive recognition by others. Watch a two-year-old play for a few minutes and you will see just how early that desire for attention shows up. "I won't lie," says Nordeman, "it feels alright to see your name in lights / We all need an 'Atta boy' or 'Atta girl.'" As we get older, that desire only grows, and glory can become a key motivation in our lives.

As Christians, we still have these same desires for recognition. But when we look at this attention from Christ's perspective, we will realize that the glory we gain on earth doesn't amount to much. Nordeman sings about this as she continues:

> You could take my picture and hang it in a gallery
> Of all the who's who and so-n-so's that used to be the best
> At such and such . . .

When you look at the world around you, notice how much value people place in making a name for themselves and being remembered as *the best*. But when all is said and done, as Nordeman sings, all they are is just another "who's who . . . that used to be the best at such 'n such." Even when we achieve the best that the world has to offer, our legacy remains just another a picture on a wall, bust in a hall, or blurb in a book somewhere. And as much as we can allow these accomplishments to define who we are here on earth, they are meaningless in the big picture. They will only gather dust and become forgotten as time goes on.

A Legacy That Matters

Jesus Christ offers accolades to his disciples that are a far cry from those that gather dust or turn to rust. Christ wants us to receive this recognition for living lives of eternal significance, spending our time on things that matter for all time. In the chorus of "Legacy," Nordeman describes how we can build this kind of legacy:

I want to leave a legacy.
How will they remember me?
Did I choose to love? Did I point to You enough
To make a mark on things?
I want to leave an offering
A child of mercy and grace who blessed Your name unapologetically
And leave that kind of legacy.

Nordeman is asking a question that everyone asks of himself or herself: *when I die, how will I be remembered?* Will you be remembered for your worldly accomplishments? Or for how you loved, shared God's grace, and worshiped the Lord? As Nordeman sings, this is the kind of thing an eternal legacy is built upon.

In "Hallelujah," the Newsboys provide a similar description of what building a legacy in heaven is like. As the song begins, they sing about a girl who is rock solid in her faith; she knows "no doubt and you can see it in her eyes." Her faith is woven into every part of her life. She praises God throughout the day "even without letting out a word to be heard." She looks toward Christ "in every single situation." And, as the chorus adds, her faith "has colored all she does and taints the way she loves."

When we hear Nichole Nordeman and the Newsboys sing about this kind of faith, we shouldn't believe it comes naturally to us. Living out our faith in this way is radical. Jesus Christ doesn't want us to simply put on a Christian hat as we work toward earthly glory like everyone else. Instead, Christ wants us to be sold out for him—to take our lives down a completely different path than we would without faith. Author Oswald Chambers once wrote about his dream of having a group of Christians living for future glory with this kind of radical faith:

> I have a great vision of a [Christian] movement where people of ability who could obviously make their living fair and flourishing in other domains, deliberately refuse to do it and live for Him alone going the world over for Him.[1]

Chambers perfectly captures the essence of what living for future glory is all about: deliberately refusing earthly recognition and significance in order to live and work for Jesus Christ instead. An eternal legacy, therefore, means risking anonymity, poverty, and insignificance for the sake of the gospel.

Challenges

Building an eternal legacy, however, can seem like swimming against a swift current. And when we make the commitment to do so, we will encounter several challenges along the way. The Newsboys sing about this reality in the second verse of "Hallelujah":

Step into the spotlight—so bright
A character check in the dead of night
To cut the stays of reason, till death defy
All understanding in the neighbor's eye
To run the race like this day's the last
celebrate
In all we do and all we say look up
'Cause the world looks on

In this verse, the Newsboys point out five challenges we will encounter when we decide to live for future, rather than earthly, glory.

Life and Meaning

First, we will experience temptation. If we are lukewarm Christians focused on the things of this world, we can live much of our lives under Satan's radar, so to speak. Satan won't have to pay much attention because we are already halfway down his path all on our own. But when we commit to building a legacy in heaven, we will "step into the spotlight" of Satan that is "so bright." We will become a prime target for him. And he's going to do everything he can to get us sidetracked in the here and now.

Second, we will be tested by God. While God will never tempt us, he will place a "character check in the dead of night" in our path. Our grit and determination are going to be tested as God seeks to mature and complete our faith. As a result, we shouldn't be taken off guard when we encounter hard times. Instead, we should be prepared to respond to them in a manner worthy of our calling.

Third, we will need to persevere even when common sense says doing so is foolish. As we live for future glory, we will find ourselves in situations that, to borrow the Newsboys' words, "cut the stays of reason" and "defy all understanding in the neighbor's eye." God will put us in those kinds of situations so he can strengthen our faith and our trust in him rather than in common sense.

> *Jesus was teaching that we are going to be held accountable for how well or poorly we made use of our time and talents*

Fourth, we are called to live to the hilt. Missionary Jim Elliot once said, "Wherever you are, be all there. Live to the hilt every situation you believe to be the will of God."[2] That's exactly the kind of attitude the Newsboys are singing about when they call on us to "run the race like this day's the last" and "celebrate in all we do and all we say." So many Christians today lead timid, defeated lives spent on avoiding risk and possible danger. Instead, Christ challenges us in the Great Commission (see Matt. 28:18–20) and his call to discipleship (see Mark 8:34–36) to build our legacies as we "live to the hilt," going the world over for him.

Fifth, we are called to be witnesses to others. The most important legacy we can leave behind is the people we bring to Jesus Christ. Therefore, as the Newsboys say, "look up 'cause the world looks on." If we crumble during times of temptation or testing, no one is going to be impressed by the reality of our faith. But as we stand firm and live life to the hilt, others can't help but take notice of our faith and recognize the truth behind it.

Day of Days

When worldly recognition and attention are so glamorous and appealing, an eternal prize can seem like something that's too far in the future to think about. But both of these songs tell us to hold tight because an incredible moment awaits us if we are faithful. Throughout "Legacy" and "Hallelujah," Nichole Nordeman and the Newsboys both look toward that "day of days" that awaits every Christian.

Jesus tells the "parable of the talents" in Matthew 25. In the story, a master gives his servants money and commands them to use it wisely while he is away. When the master returns, he finds that two servants invested their talents and made money for the master, while one servant was too fearful of losing it and simply buried his money. The servants who invested wisely are praised by the master, who tells each of them, "Well done, good and faithful servant" (vv. 21, 23). However, the one who responded poorly was told, "You wicked, lazy servant!" (v. 26). In this parable, Jesus was teaching that we are going to be held accountable for how well or poorly we made use of our time and talents while living on earth.

Consequently, when all is said and done with your life, only six words are going to matter. Are you going to hear those words—*"Well done, good and faithful servant"*—spoken from the mouth of God? As Nordeman sings in the bridge of "Legacy," everything else we can do with our lives pales in comparison:

> Not well traveled, not well read, not well-to-do or well bred
> Just want to hear instead, "Well done," good and faithful one

The Newsboys also build momentum through the entire song of "Hallelujah" for that moment when we meet God in heaven and hear those words:

> We're waiting for the day
> We'll hear the Father say
> Yeah, to hear him say
> "Well done, good and faithful one
> Enter in, come on, share with me
> Welcome home, good and faithful one
> On and on through eternity..."

On that day of days, just a few spoken words will sum up your entire life. They will reveal whether your legacy was eternal or you were preoccupied with the temporary trappings of this world.

Eric Liddell and Pete Rose looked for glory in far different places. Even today, Rose continues to cling to his hope for the "immortality" of one day having his bust appear in the National Baseball Hall of Fame and Museum in Cooperstown, New York.

Eric Liddell, however, always had his sights set far higher. He knew what real immortality was all about, and he wouldn't let anything sidetrack him.

In fact, Eric Liddell is known today less for his running ability than for his courageous refusal to run at the 1924 Olympic Games. As memorably depicted in the Oscar-winning film *Chariots of Fire*, Liddell refused to run in the opening heats of the 100-meter race because they were scheduled for a Sunday. To Liddell, Sunday was for God, not racing, and not even pressure from the future king of England could change his mind. If another British runner had not graciously let Liddell take his place in the 400-meter event, Liddell never would have even competed in the Olympics. But had that happened, he would have been just fine. When everything was on the line, he proved less interested in a gold medal than in the only legacy and glory that truly matter.

In "Legacy" and "Hallelujah," Nichole Nordeman and the Newsboys sing of that future time and place when you will meet God face-to-face. That meeting is a certainty. Only a single question remains until that time arrives: how is God going to respond to you?

Life and Meaning

LEGACY
by Nichole Nordeman

I don't mind if you've got something nice
   to say about me
And I enjoy an accolade like the rest.
You could take my picture and hang it in a
   gallery
Of all the who's who and so-n-so's that
   used to be the best
At such and such . . . it wouldn't matter
   much

I won't lie, it feels alright to see your name
   in lights
We all need an "Atta boy" or "Atta girl."
But in the end I'd like to hang my hat on
   more besides
The temporary trappings of this world.

[Chorus:]
I want to leave a legacy.
How will they remember me?
Did I choose to love? Did I point to You
   enough

To make a mark on things?
I want to leave an offering.
A child of mercy and grace who blessed
Your name unapologetically.
And leave that kind of legacy.

I don't have to look too far or too long
   awhile
To make a lengthy list of all that I enjoy.
It's an accumulating trinket and a treasure
   pile
Where moth and rust, thieves and such will
   soon enough destroy.

[Chorus]

Not well traveled, not well read, not well-
   to-do or well bred
Just want to hear instead, "Well done,"
   good and faithful one . . .

HALLELUJAH
by the Newsboys

Walk into the sunlight so bright
Illumination blocking out night
She knows that the promises are airtight
There is no doubt and you can see it in her
   eyes

You'll hear her singing to heaven—even
Without letting out a word to be heard
In every single situation (none too big—
   none too small)
She looks up and the world looks on

[Chorus:]
She sings hallelujah
When all has become nothing
And her hope in the savior
Has colored all she does
And taints the way she loves

She sings hallelujah
And falls to the ground again
With hands stretched up to the sky
Waiting for the day
She'll hear the father say . . .

Step into the spotlight—so bright
A character check in the dead of night
To cut the stays of reason, till death defy
All understanding in the neighbor's eye
To run the race like this day's the last
   celebrate
In all we do and all we say look up
'Cause the world looks on

[Chorus]

We sing hallelujah
When all has become nothing
And our hope in the savior
Has colored all we do
Let it be for you

We'll sing hallelujah
And fall to the ground again
With hands stretched up to the sky
We're waiting for the day
We'll hear the father say
Yeah, to hear him say
"Well done, good and faithful one
Enter in, come on, share with me
Welcome home, good and faithful one
On and on through eternity . . ."

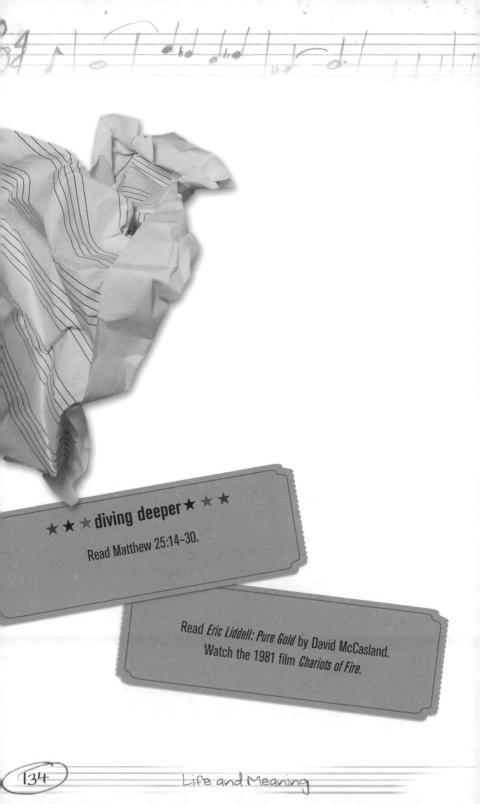

Read Matthew 25:14–30.

Read *Eric Liddell: Pure Gold* by David McCasland.
Watch the 1981 film *Chariots of Fire*.

Action Steps

Nichole Nordeman in her song "Legacy" and the Newsboys in "Hallelujah" sing of the future glory that awaits Christians who live a life worthy of their calling. As you think about the legacy you are building, consider the following steps:

Take stock of where your heart is. Are you building a legacy in heaven? Or are you setting your sights too low and settling for earthly glory that will eventually fade away? Make the gutsy decisions that honor Christ, even as you risk anonymity and poverty in the here and now.

Avoid putting a Christian wrapper onto your earthly dreams and goals. God wants you to live sold out for him, not to do whatever you want while you wear a Christian hat. That doesn't mean that God never wants you to achieve or to be recognized, but it does mean that your motivation needs to be serving him, not yourself. Spend some time in prayer asking God to show you any selfish motives you may have.

Watch the film Chariots of Fire with an eye on how Eric Liddell kept the Olympics in perspective with what was truly important in his life.

Part Four

The
Chris

And with my smoke-filled lungs
I cry out for freedom
While locking and chaining myself
To my rotting desires
   Caedmon's Call, "Coming Home"

When Jesus calls a man, he bids him "come and die."
      Dietrich Bonhoeffer, The Cost of Discipleship

11
Earplugs

Imagine that as you walk along a beach, you discover a mysterious oil lamp half-buried in the sand. You pick it up and dust it off. Just for fun, you start to rub the lamp gently with your hands. But suddenly, to your shock and amazement, a genie pops out. The genie is so excited about his newfound freedom that he offers to grant you a wish as a thank-you gift. Images of money, cars, and Hollywood fame rush through your head in your frantic excitement. But after you calm down and start to agonize over your choice, the disciple in you eventually wins out. You decide to wish for something even more priceless than money or fame: to clearly hear God's voice and know exactly what his will is for your life.

Many Christians would jump into their cars and dash off to the nearest beach if they thought they could hear God speak simply by finding a magic lamp. Indeed, the great mystery in the life of a believer is hearing God. I know friends who have read a shelf of books on how to listen to God's voice and know God's will—yet when I ask them for the inside scoop, their typical reaction resembles a deer staring into headlights.

Trying to hear God's voice in a world without burning bushes can leave us scratching our heads.

Hearing God has not always been this hard, at least for some believers. The Bible reports times when God talked to people like Abraham, Moses, Elijah, and Paul. He used a variety of ways to speak to them—a burning bush, a voice from the sky, and messenger angels, to name a few. But no matter how he spoke, the message was always loud, clear, and decisive. Obviously, God doesn't make it a habit to send the same audible messages to

Christians today as he did to those few biblical heroes. No megaphones are blaring from the clouds, though God does promise that the direction he does provide is more than enough to live faithfully as a disciple.

God's guarantee, however, does not mean that figuring out what he is saying is a no-brainer. As Chris Rice sings about in "Smell the Color 9," trying to hear God's voice in a world without burning bushes can leave us scratching our heads. We can feel as if we are wearing earplugs that prevent God's message from coming through. In this song, Rice explores the mystery of hearing God, and he concludes that a life of faith perseveres even when God's voice is silent or unclear.

Headaches

Whether we are a newbie Christian or a longtime believer, hearing God's clear direction for our lives can be a frustrating challenge. Chris Rice identifies with that frustration as he starts off "Smell the Color 9." In the opening lines, he says what is on the minds of many Christians:

> I would take no for an answer
> Just to know I heard You speak

Many of us, like Rice, desire to follow God's will for our lives. But as we seek God's direction, we would like to be certain that we are headed the right way, to have a quiet confidence that we are not misinterpreting his signs. We pray about major decisions in our lives—whether or not we should go to college, take that new job, accept a marriage proposal, or go into ministry. As we do so, God's leading may crystallize in our hearts immediately. But other times, God seems to be MIA. This period of uneasy silence can drive us nuts. The waiting game takes on a life of its own and starts to seem far worse than a negative response from God. In fact, we'd honestly prefer to "take no for an answer" just so we could be 100 percent certain of God's will for our lives.

God's silence can seem unfair when we are trying to give our lives to Jesus Christ and live out his call to "take up your cross and follow him" (Mark 8:34). After all, we humans are deal makers. If we make a deal with someone, we expect something in return. We can fall into the trap of applying this same logic to our relationship with God: we give a decision over to him, but in response we expect a clear message as to what our choice should be. The result is that if confirmation never seems to come, we either turn on God or on ourselves. We can start to believe God has let us down and is not living up to his end of the deal. Or we can start to believe something is wrong with us—that we are not hearing his voice or are misinterpreting what he is trying to tell us.

What Rice is suggesting in this song, however, is that perhaps we face neither of these problems. Maybe sometimes, because we are human, we just cannot figure out God. Isaiah 55:8 confirms this idea: "'My thoughts are not your thoughts, neither are your ways my ways,' declares the Lord." That is exactly the point Chris Rice is stressing when he says at the end of the first verse:

> But sometimes finding You
> Is just like trying to
> Smell the color nine

Smell the color nine? You may be wondering what Rice could possi-

Some Christians talk quite boldly about being able to listen to God's voice.

The Christian Walk

bly mean. He offers an explanation in the closing lines of the song:

Smell the color nine?
But nine's not a color
And even if it were, you can't smell a color
That's my point exactly

Obviously, "smelling the color nine" not only does not make sense but is also impossible. In fact, if you spend too much time trying to analyze that phrase, you will probably get a migraine headache. In the same way, sometimes when we try to hear God or know his will, it seems not only confusing and illogical but ultimately impossible to understand. That's because we are finite creatures, while God is infinite. We look at the here and now, but God sees eternity. We know a little; God knows all. Given the fact that we aren't equals with God, our understanding is never going to completely line up with God's: we simply aren't sufficiently equipped for the task.

Attempts

Our minds may spin when we attempt to hear God, but not everyone seems to have that same trouble. Indeed, some Christians talk quite boldly about being able to listen to God's voice. This confidence usually flows from their claims to hear God in two distinct ways.

Some Christians listen for God's voice through special revelations. They look at what God did in biblical times and expect that same kind of experience with God today: hearing an actual voice from God, looking for a visible sign, or maybe even witnessing a supernatural event. "God told me" is a common expression heard from this camp. Chris Rice compares himself to others who claim these kind of experiences. He wonders why he's "never seen the signs they claim to see," adding that he's never "felt the presence" or "heard the calling." When we hear someone making such claims, we may ask ourselves, as Rice does, "Are the special revelations meant for everybody but me?"

Other Christians focus on hearing God's voice through human effort. In the second verse of "Smell the Color 9," Chris Rice contrasts his own experience with this mind-set:

'Cause I can sniff, I can see
I can count up pretty high
But these faculties aren't getting me
Any closer to the sky

When we begin to think that hearing God is possible using our own "faculties," we start to believe that knowing God's will can be reduced to a formula—*Know God's will in five easy steps. Don't delay. Call today.* Many well-intentioned Christian authors and preachers border on falling into this trap.

No matter how we listen for God's voice, however, we must make sure we pay attention to what Chris Rice is saying in this song: don't fool yourself into believing that you can actually "smell the color nine." God cannot be put into a box and be expected to behave as we predict.

Even If

If we struggle to hear God's voice, it can be a real downer to talk to someone who thinks they have it all figured out. We can be looked upon with a scowl. Our Christian faith questioned. Hidden sins assumed. A best-selling Christian book even goes so far as to question a person's very salvation if God's voice does not hit them over the head with a clear message. In "Smell the Color 9," Chris Rice toys with that perspective as he wonders, "Maybe I don't truly know You." But, as if thinking further, he follows that up with an alternative thought: "Or maybe I just simply believe."

This "simply believing" from the song is exactly the kind of faith that Shadrach, Meshach, and Abednego had. As reported in the book of Daniel, these three young Israelites were put into a scorching furnace because they refused to bow down to an idol constructed by King Nebuchadnezzar. Just before they were forced into the fire, the trio were questioned by the king about their refusal. They responded by saying they were confident that if they were to be thrown into the furnace, God would save them from it. But, not stopping there, the trio added, "But even if he does not, we want you to know, O king, that we will not serve your gods" (Dan. 3:18). That "simply believing" attitude that Shadrach, Meshach, and Abednego had demonstrates the heart of a true disciple. True disciples do not lose their faith at times when God is silent. Even if God doesn't talk, they still believe.

Rice sings of this type of simple faith. In spite of the fact that you may not get special revelations from God, your "heart of faith keeps poundin'." And as the second verse continues, Rice emphasizes the most important request that a true disciple asks of God:

So I'm not looking for burning bushes
Or some divine graffiti to appear
I'm just begging You for some wisdom
And believing You're putting some here

True faith does not depend on seeing "burning bushes" or "divine graffiti." Instead, the disciple's desire is simply the wisdom to discern God's will even when hearing his voice is difficult.

Seeking Wisdom

Since God's ways are not our ways, how can we receive that wisdom that Rice is begging for? While there are no formulas, we can apply three biblical principles to our Christian walk. By following these we are not guaranteed when or how God will respond, but each of them will prepare our hearts and mold us to be able to better listen to God's voice.

First, we can hear God by diving into his Word. At first glance, reading a book written thousands of years ago may not sound too relevant when we want to know what to do today. But as the book of Hebrews says, the Bible is a living and breathing book (see Heb. 4:12). As a result, the Bible can speak to you as much nowadays as it did to its readers the day it was penned. God's Word is an ever-changing book that continually adapts itself to our situations: we can get something out of a passage the first time we read it, then go back later and have something new leap off the same page. Psalm 119:105 adds that God's Word is a lamp to our feet and a light for our path. As a result, we can use the Bible as a road map in our Christian walk.

While God empowers his written Word to continually speak new truth to us, he also uses his Word to teach us who he is. If, for example, you are struggling to hear God on a major decision, you can read about what is important to him and apply those principles to the choice you are trying to make. Or suppose you are struggling with whether God would approve of you participating in a questionable activity. As you read about God's holiness, you begin to understand that he would never approve of you doing anything that even hints at sin. Finally, when you read the way Jesus spoke to the Pharisees, you can discover how much more concerned God is about your heart condition than he is about your following rules and regulations.

Second, we can hear God's voice through prayer. Prayer is nothing more complicated than a conversation with God, just like we can have with a best friend. On the surface, the conversation seems like a one-sided affair, but it really is not. God does use prayer to communicate to us. That doesn't mean that we are going to hear an audible voice or feel a tingle in our stomach. However, the more we pray and open up to God, the more he will, in some unexplainable way, make his presence and will known to us.

Third, we can listen to God's voice through the Holy Spirit who lives inside of us. Jesus promised that when we become born again, the Holy Spirit comes to work inside of us. One of his primary missions as he lives in us is correcting and convicting us. In fact, the Holy Spirit is even referred to by poet Francis Thompson as the "Hound of Heaven." Like a hound dog, he is relentless in his pursuit of us, not letting up until we surrender. A second way in which the Holy Spirit helps us know God's will is by arranging circumstances in our lives and guiding our paths. As the life of the apostle Paul (see Acts 16) demonstrates, if we are focused on following God, the Holy Spirit will lead us and direct our paths.

When it comes to living out these principles on a practical, day-in, day-out basis, Oswald Chambers had a great way of look-ing at life. His lifelong motto was "Trust God and do the next thing." Chambers believed God is intimately involved in the lives of Christians, busy engineering circumstances all around us. But, at the same time, Chambers did not think that we should sit with our hands tied behind our backs until we hear a booming voice from the clouds. His conviction was that if we are genuinely living as disciples, our lives are usually going to be in line with

God's will. A Christian, therefore, simply needs to trust and go. If we head down the wrong route, the "Hound of Heaven" will correct us and gently guide us back to the right path. When we trust God and do the next thing, we are able to live a life like Chris Rice talks about at the end of the last verse:

And I've never "heard the calling"
But somehow You've led me right here

These key lines of the song offer a clue as to why hearing God can be such a mystery. Perhaps the reason that God does not always communicate clearly is not out of neglect but out of *purpose*. Think back to what Jesus told his disciples after his resurrection: "Because you have seen me, you have believed; blessed are those who have not seen and yet have believed" (John 20:29). Evidently the type of disciples that God wants to shape and mold in today's world are those who do not need to see or hear before believing. In the end, what God wants most is for us to carry on our faith even when doing so makes as much sense as "smelling the color nine."

SMELL THE COLOR 9
by Chris Rice

I would take no for an answer
Just to know I heard You speak
And I'm wonderin' why I've never
Seen the signs they claim to see
Are the special revelations
Meant for everybody but me?
Maybe I don't truly know You
Or maybe I just simply believe

[Chorus:]
'Cause I can sniff, I can see
I can count up pretty high
But these faculties aren't getting me
Any closer to the sky
But my heart of faith keeps poundin'
So I know I'm doin' fine
But sometimes finding You
Is just like trying to
Smell the color nine

Now I've never "felt the presence"
But I know You're always near
And I've never "heard the calling"
But somehow You've led me right here
So I'm not looking for burning bushes
Or some divine graffiti to appear
I'm just begging You for some wisdom
And believing You're putting some here

[Chorus]

Smell the color nine?
But nine's not a color
And even if it were, you can't smell a color
That's my point exactly

★ ★ ★ **diving deeper** ★ ★ ★
Read Isaiah 55:8–9; Daniel 3; John 14:16–18;
and Hebrews 4:12.

Action Steps

In "Smell the Color 9," Chris Rice talks about how hard hearing God's voice or knowing his will can be. As you try to hear God, consider the following steps:

Seek to hear God by reading his Word, praying to him daily and being receptive to the Holy Spirit in your life. Don't look for God's voice through "burning bushes" or through canned formulas ("Knowing God's will in three easy steps," etc.)

In your Bible reading look for examples of God using times of uncertainty or silence to shape and mold his followers into the kind of people he wanted them to be.

When you face an uncertain situation and are not sure where God is leading you, begin by asking him to guide you and then take the first step that seems consistent with what God would want. Ask God for wisdom and proceed one step at a time. As you "trust God and do the next thing" he will lead you to where he wants, encouraging you as proceed down the right path or correcting you when you go astray.

12

Nagging Doubts

I wished to be made just as certain of things that I could not see, as I was certain that seven and three make ten.

Saint Augustine

Growing up in a Christian home, I became a born-again believer at the ripe young age of eight. During my preteen and teenage years, I never had doubts or questioned God—I just assumed Christianity was true because that was what I was taught. However, when I went off to college, misgivings and uncertainty began to creep into my head for the first time. Does God really exist? If so, why doesn't he reveal himself more clearly? How could God really love the world and allow bad things to happen? I began to wonder whether the faith I had always relied upon was true or just a fairy tale.

As time passed, I didn't know what to do with this uncertainty. I had never heard any other Christian talk much about doubt before. I assumed other Christians believed without questioning. By comparison, I concluded something must be wrong with my faith: why was I asking questions about issues no one else around me seemed to have problems with?

Looking back today at that time in my life, I can see that the honest questioning I went through was a turning point for my faith. As I continued to seek Jesus Christ in the midst of uncertainty, my paper-thin faith was slowly transformed into something far more solid. Philip Yancey describes what happened to me when he says, "Relationships gain strength when they are stretched to the breaking point and don't break."[1]

Perhaps doubt is a natural part of the faith-building process.

The Christian Walk

Chris Rice in "Big Enough" and Caedmon's Call in "Prove Me Wrong" focus on the struggle of doubts rising up in our Christian life. Both songs are prayers, crying out to God for answers to the nagging doubts that can threaten to drive us away from him.

The "D" Word

If you walk into a typical church on Sunday mornings, chances are that you will hear plenty of sermons about encouragement and God's blessings and sing such hymns as "Blessed Assurance" and "Trust and Obey." But few, if any, churches will utter the dreaded "D" word—*doubt*—from the pulpit. Many Christians clam up when this word is mentioned. Some argue it is not a problem for serious believers. Others, scared of having their beliefs questioned, shy away from even thinking about it. Still others consider doubt a sin, something that one should flee from like one would flee from lust or lying.

The "D" word is nothing new to God's people, however, and the Bible certainly does not shy away from talking about it. Scripture holds many accounts of brutally honest believers who question God and plead with him for answers. Psalm 10:1 asks, "Why, O LORD, do you stand far off? Why do you hide yourself in times of trouble?" Three chapters later, David continues, saying, "How long, O LORD? Will you forget me forever?" (Ps. 13:1). "The LORD has forsaken me," adds Isaiah 49:14; "the Lord has forgotten me." By reading the Bible, we can see that God never tries to suggest that every believer will experience a 100 Percent Certified Doubt-Free Christian Life. Jesus does say in John 20:29, "Blessed are those who have not seen and yet have believed." But at the same time, he seems to take for granted that we will go through times of struggle, doubt, and questioning. Perhaps doubt is a natural part of the faith-building process.

As Chris Rice starts off "Big Enough," he reveals the thoughts that echo through our minds when we question God. The first verse goes:

None of us knows and this makes it a mystery
If life is a comedy, then why all the tragedy?
Three and a half pounds of brain try to
    figure out
What this world is all about
And is there an eternity
Is there an eternity?

As Rice shows, the Christian faith has an element of mystery to it. **Every Christian can be confident of the truth of Christianity.** God provides us with signposts—such as the Bible, his creation, our consciences, and our rational minds—that point us toward him. But we still cannot see God with our eyes; we cannot serve up irrefutable proof. As a result, some aspects of Christianity will always remain a "mystery" as long as we walk this earth. "Doubt always coexists with faith," Philip Yancey reminds us. "For in the presence of certainty who would need faith at all?"[2]

Since mystery remains, God's actions can seem suspicious to us and become a stumbling block to our faith. If God is loving and fully in control of all things, then, in the words of Chris Rice, "why all this tragedy?" We can find it terribly hard to accept that God allows tragic events to go on without stopping them, particularly when they happen to us or someone we love.

Questions flow not only through our minds but into our hearts as well. We can wonder whether God really loves us, whether he is going to care for us like he promises. Caedmon's Call sings about this fear in the first verse of "Prove Me Wrong":

The Christian Walk

Sometimes I fear maybe I'm not chosen
You've hardened my heart like Pharaoh
And that would explain why life is so hard for
me

As the apostle Paul alludes to in Romans 9, God hardened the heart of Pharaoh, the Egyptian ruler who refused Moses's command to let the Israelite slaves go from Egypt. God took this action as a judgment for Pharaoh's continued, longtime disobedience, particularly when God revealed himself clearly to Pharaoh on several occasions. In the same way, we may sometimes feel like our "life is so hard" that God must be dealing with us like he did with Pharaoh.

When we question God in our heads or hearts, the "D" word begins to take root. Chris Rice wonders, "Is there an eternity?" and "Does anyone hear us pray?" Caedmon's Call confesses, "I fear maybe this is all just a game."

If you struggle with doubt and ask these kinds of questions, realize you are not alone. C. S. Lewis was one of the most influential Christian authors to provide strong intellectual arguments for the existence of God and the truth of Christianity. Yet even he had occasional problems with doubt, particularly when his wife died of cancer just three years after he married her. In a letter to a close friend, Lewis confessed that he had no rational reason for doubting. However, he had a lot of baggage that dragged him down—his skeptical personality, the cynicism of modern society, and the circumstances he sometimes found himself in. In his words, they "steal away all my lively feeling of the truth, and often when I pray I wonder if I am not posting letters to a non-existent address."[3] However, Lewis came to realize that his doubts are more emotional than anything else:

"Mind you, I don't think [my beliefs are false]—the whole of my reasonable mind is convinced: but I often *feel* so."[4]

Honest Fears

When we battle uncertainty, we are to do as Chris Rice and Caedmon's Call do—be honest with God about it. Don't try to sweep your fears under the rug, and don't try to ignore God. Chris Rice expresses the kind of honest prayers that every Christian should offer when they are struggling:

> God, if You're there, I wish You'd show me
> And God, if You care, then I need You to know me
> I hope You don't mind me asking the questions
> But I figure You're big enough
> I figure You're big enough

We can question God, not out of disrespect but because we know who we are in relation to him. Each of us is a sinful, flawed creature compared to a mighty and holy God. But God doesn't mind it. As Rice sings, God is "big enough" to handle what you can throw at him.

Both Rice and Caedmon's Call emphasize the helplessness they feel when they are in this battle. Rice feels unable to deal with it and cries out for God to handle his doubts. "I figure You're big enough," says Rice. Caedmon's Call echoes this same feeling of helplessness in the chorus of "Prove Me Wrong":

> Cast out my doubts, please prove me wrong
> 'Cause these demons can be so headstrong

Make my walls fall, please prove me wrong
'Cause this resentment's been building
Burn them up with your fire so strong
And if you can before I Baal, please prove me wrong

Like Caedmon's Call, ask God to get rid of all the doubts you struggle with. Cry out to him to cast them out, make the walls fall, and prove you wrong. Doubts are powerful enemies to conquer and cannot be stopped on your own. In the chorus of "Prove Me Wrong," Caedmon's Call pleads with God to remove their doubts before they bail out on God. The line "If you can before I Baal" is a wordplay. It refers to the story of Elijah on Mount Carmel, found in 1 Kings 18, in which God showed his power over the false god Baal by burning a water-soaked altar. Caedmon's Call asks the Lord to burn up their doubts with the same fire before they give up on God and turn somewhere else.

Pressing On

Neither Chris Rice nor Caedmon's Call tries to provide any pat, happy-face answers as they conclude their songs. Both "Big Enough" and "Prove Me Wrong" end with questions and heartfelt cries for answers. In the same way, as we struggle and find answers slow in coming, we can make Caedmon's Call's prayer our own: "Keep me still until the day you prove me wrong." As we look for that patience, we can follow the models of Psalm 13 and Isaiah 40.

Psalm 13 is a good place to turn to when we feel like giving up. David, author of this six-verse psalm, starts off by questioning God and pleading with him for help: "How long, O LORD? Will you forget me forever? How long will you hide your face from me? How long must I wrestle with my thoughts and every day have sorrow in my heart? . . . Look on me and answer, O

LORD my God" (vv. 1–3). As the psalm concludes, however, David suddenly switches tone. He makes no mention of any earth-shattering revelations or answers, but he is now able to find peace through a simple trust. He ends the psalm with: "But I trust in your unfailing love; my heart rejoices in your salvation. I will sing to the LORD, for he has been good to me" (vv. 5–6). David knew the character of God. Therefore, he could continue to trust the Lord even in the midst of hardship.

One of the most quoted chapters in the Old Testament, Isaiah 40, has long been used as a passage of encouragement. It highlights how actively involved God is in the lives of people who believe in him. Isaiah writes, "Those who hope in the LORD will renew their strength. They will soar on wings like eagles; they will run and not grow weary, they will walk and not be faint" (Isa. 40:31). When we read these verses alone, they sound much like a pep talk to people already confident in God. Yet reading those verses in context reveals that nothing could be further from the truth. Back up a few verses and we see that those words are not for a group of victorious believers. They were directed at a defeated people struggling with doubt and disillusionment. Isaiah pointed them back to who God was and then proceeded with the incredible promise that they will "run and not grow weary" (v. 31).

Both Chris Rice in "Big Enough" and Caedmon's Call in "Prove Me Wrong" ask probing questions of God and wonder whether God can be trusted. But as you listen to the struggles showcased in both songs, keep in mind the lesson of Psalm 13 and Isaiah 40: if you know God's character and cling to it, your trust and hope *will* survive.

In the end, perhaps living the life of faith in the midst of uncertainty is best described by poet T. S. Elliot: "Only hints and guesses, hints followed by guesses . . . the rest is prayer, observance, discipline, thought, and action."[5]

BIG ENOUGH
by Chris Rice

None of us knows and that makes it a
  mystery
If life is a comedy, then why all the tragedy?
Three and a half pounds of brain try to
  figure out
What this world is all about
And is there an eternity
Is there an eternity?

[Chorus:]
God, if You're there, I wish You'd show me
And God, if You care, then I need You to
  know me
I hope You don't mind me asking the
  questions
But I figure You're big enough
I figure You're big enough

Lying on pillows we're haunted and half-
  awake
Does anyone hear us pray, "If I die before I
  wake"?
Then the morning comes and the mirror's
  another place
Where we wrestle face to face
With the image of deity
The image of deity

[Chorus]

When I imagine the size of the universe
And I wonder what's out past the edges
Then I discover inside me a space as big
And believe that I'm meant to be
Filled up with more than just questions

Used by permission. 14

PROVE ME WRONG
by Caedmon's Call

Sometimes I fear maybe I'm not chosen
You've hardened my heart like Pharaoh
And that would explain why life is so hard
  for me

And I am sad Esau hated
Crying against what's faded
Saying father, please, is there any left for
  me

[Chorus:]
Cast out my doubts, please prove me
  wrong
'Cause these demons can be so headstrong
Make my walls fall, please prove me wrong
'Cause this resentment's been building
Burn them up with your fire so strong
If you can before I Baal, please prove me
  wrong

I fear maybe this is all just a game
Our friends and our families all play too
Harness the young and give some comfort
  to the old

[Chorus]

Don't let my doubts prove true
Draw me close and hold me near to you
Keep me strong until the day you

[Chorus]

Used by permission. 15

Action Steps

Chris Rice in "Big Enough" and Caedmon's Call in "Prove Me Wrong" both deal with the struggles Christians have with doubt and questioning God. If you struggle in this area, take the following steps to strengthen your faith:

Read through the book of Psalms and join in as the writer sometimes questions or argues with God but ultimately puts his trust in the Lord.

Read The Problem of Pain by C. S. Lewis. You may find the book tough at times, particularly the first chapter or two, but hardly any book is better at showing how God uses suffering for his purposes.

When you pray, be honest with God. Don't try to ignore the problem or put on a fake smile. God wants you to be real with him.

★ ★ ★ **diving deeper** ★ ★ ★

Read Psalms 10; 13; Isaiah 40:27-31; 49:14; and Romans 9.

13

Sin Traps

"I'm free! I'm free!" shouted a young boy running across the grassy yard of a first-century farm. As he wildly flapped his arms, the boy looked ready to soar high in the air. But on the far side of the yard, a down-and-out farm laborer named Jonathan looked on with no thought of leaving the ground. Busily feeding the pigs in the pigpen, Jonathan shook his head in disgust, muttering, "Be careful what you wish for, boy. You just might get it."

Jonathan straightened up to watch the boy buzz around until he was out of sight, then gazed across the lonely, muddy pen surrounding him. *How did my dream life,* he wondered, *turn into this rotten nightmare?* His question carried his thoughts back to the time months earlier when, in a big-time act of defiance, he had demanded his share of his dad's inheritance. Little details like his father still being alive didn't seem to faze him at the time. Jonathan remembered speaking the same words as the boy—"I'm free! I'm free!"—when he shook the dirt of his hometown off of his sandals and set off for a life of adventure.

His plan was simple: find happiness and meaning by doing what he wanted, when he wanted, not how his father wanted him to do things. And for a while, everything seemed to work. Life was great. He was hanging out with the in crowd, buying fancy clothes, and living in luxury. But as the months wore on, he slowly found himself becoming a slave to his bad habits and developed an endless desire for *more.* More drink. More food. More clothes. More women. More anything.

But when a famine and hard times came around in the country, his wild lifestyle quickly ate up the rest of his

"Coming Home" reveals a wonderful promise from Jesus Christ if we choose to return to him and leave our sin behind.

The Christian Walk

cash. Before long Jonathan found himself broke, homeless, hungry, and alone. He didn't know where to turn, but going back home to his father was unthinkable. So in one last desperate attempt to save himself, he found a job as a lowly farm worker, feeding pigs.

Looking back, it seemed that every plan he had made turned out to be a cruel joke played on him. His giant leap for freedom crash-landed into this muddy, slimy pigpen.

Shaking out of his daze, Jonathan leaned over and resumed his job of feeding the pigs. But as he did so, a pig making a bee-line for the feed trough bumped into his leg, sending Jonathan face-first into the mud. Jumping up in a rage, Jonathan cursed and screamed to himself, trying rather unsuccessfully to wipe the mud from his face.

"What am I doing here? Enough of this!" Jonathan muttered to himself. "I'm going home."

In perhaps the most famous of all his parables, Jesus tells the story in Luke 15 of a young man like Jonathan who rebels against his father and leaves home to selfishly live out his life on his own terms. Using the symbolism of the prodigal son as a backdrop to their song "Coming Home," Caedmon's Call talks about how everyday Christians can get themselves in the same sin trap that took down the prodigal. But, like the parable, "Coming Home" also reveals a wonderful promise from Jesus Christ if we choose to return to him and leave our sin behind: he will run to us and welcome us home.

The "Almost" Sacrifice

The apostle Paul, in his letter to the Roman Christians, calls on Christians to offer their bodies as "living sacrifices" (Rom. 12:1). But as I reflect on that word *sacrifice*, I am not sure if many

Christians nowadays really get it. Perhaps we'll sacrifice listening to secular music or go without chocolate during Lent. Or, if we are really missions-minded, we'll give up a Coke a day to support a third world child. Don't get me wrong, these activities may be worthwhile and pleasing to God. But more often than not, the concept of "sacrifice" can be dumbed down to mean nothing more than a temporary or minor hardship. The original readers of Romans, however, would have grasped a much deeper meaning in Paul's words. You see, in the Old Testament, the Israelites were commanded to offer animal sacrifices to God. In fact, sacrifice was the most sacred act of obedience performed by the Jews.

The concept of "sacrifice" can be dumbed down to mean nothing more than a temporary or minor hardship.

Taking the life of an animal was a symbolic act for the Israelites. It was a visual reminder designed to show the price of a person's sin. The offender or priest would kill the animal, cut the body into pieces, often burn part of the sacrifice in a sacred fire, and then place all the pieces on the altar. The burnt portion was considered the greatest sacrifice and meant to express total dedication to God by the one who gave it.

But Hebrews 10:18 tells us that burnt offerings are history, a thing of the past. Burnt offerings aren't needed anymore because God himself made the ultimate sacrifice as a payment for sin: he sent his Son to the earth to be killed on the cross. As Paul indicates in Romans 12, when we begin to realize just how much God gave up for us, then the only response that makes sense is to surrender our hopes, wants, desires—everything—and become a living, ongoing sacrifice to Jesus (see Rom. 12:1–2).

Caedmon's Call starts off "Coming Home" by contrasting Paul's command to be a living sacrifice with what real life is all too often like for you and me: *saying one thing and doing another.* The first verse begins:

You say you want a living sacrifice
Well I am a burnt offering
Crawling off the altar and
Back into the fire

In a burst of emotion, it's easy to offer our lives as a living sacrifice to God. Perhaps we make that decision in a church service, at a youth group event, or on a missions trip. But once we get back into normal life, peer pressures, temptations, and compromises stare us in the face. Before long we can gradually find ourselves going back on our commitment. Once we give in to our desires, we slowly begin, as the song says, "crawling off the altar and back into the fire." But the imagery of "Coming Home" helps us see what a slap in the face that kind of "almost sacrifice" is to God: it's just like an Israelite who makes a burnt offering, lays it on the altar, and then later takes it back for himself.

When we give part but not all of ourselves to God, we'll constantly fall into traps of sin. A tug-of-war between sin and sacrifice forms in our hearts. Back and forth, the lead changes sides; we find victory for a while when we're on a spiritual high, but sin gains the upper hand when everyday life resumes. Caedmon's Call describes this see-saw battle that rages in our hearts as the first verse continues:

And with my smoke-filled lungs
I cry out for freedom

> While locking and chaining myself
> To my rotting desires
>
> And I hate the stench
> But I swallow the key

When we are trapped in sin, we'll often start to feel God's conviction and make an attempt to cry out to God for his help. But if we aren't fully committed to leaving that sin behind forever, we'll never get anywhere. Like the song says, we'll be crying out to God with our mouths while at the same time using our hands to "lock and chain" ourselves to our "rotting desires."

This tug-of-war between sin and sacrifice will leave us seasick. We begin our day convinced that we are ready to face the world, but we find ourselves falling on our faces before the sun sets. Our sin becomes something we despise and hate, but we still irrationally "swallow the key" that could release us from the prison we've built for ourselves. The apostle Paul understood exactly this clash that can rage in our hearts. In Romans 7, Paul confesses that he too sometimes doesn't understand what he finds himself doing: "For what I want to do I do not do, but what I hate I do. . . . I have the desire to do what is good, but I cannot carry it out. . . . The evil I don't want to do—this I keep on doing" (vv. 15, 18–19).

Ultimately, only when we hit bottom do we realize we can't have it both ways. Then we are much like the prodigal son when he reaches the low point in that mud pit—ready to cry out for help, ready to come home. The first verse of "Coming Home" concludes by showing the path out of this dilemma:

> And with it stuck in my throat
> Can you hear me

When we feel trapped, we can and must call out to God, even when we feel like we can't be heard because of our past actions.

Shell-Shocked

During World War I, most soldiers spent their time on the front lines in wet, mud-filled trenches. They tried their best to stay alive in the midst of daily barrages of mortar rounds, which were explosive bombshells fired toward them by the enemy on the other side. The brutal reality of trench warfare in World War I was so horrible and jarring that many soldiers experienced emotional and mental breakdowns called "shell shock." This hell on earth the soldiers faced is a powerful picture of what a Christian's battle with sin can be like. Caedmon's Call focuses on that imagery in the song's second verse:

> I am shell-shocked and I have walked
> Through the trenches full of tears
> With the mortars of memory
> Exploding in my burning ears

Walking through life as a Christian, we can easily become shell-shocked as a result of the battles we experience trying to overcome sin. Sin can haunt us. Sometimes that's because of the real-world consequences of our sin that we have to face, but that isn't what Caedmon's Call is talking about here. They are speaking of the spiritual stain of sin that can be left on our hearts. Our past failures can become "mortars of memory" that explode in our "burning ears." We can become obsessed by the feelings of failure and helplessness that result from giving in to sin. In many ways, we can feel quite like that young World

War I private living in the trenches, bracing for the next artillery attack that is expected at any moment.

Yet Christians never have to stay put in the front-line trenches of guilt. Oh, Satan wants to keep you there, as he endlessly fires off guilt-filled mortars toward you. But God will *never* haunt you with your past; when you need to confess and repent of your sins, God produces in you something called godly sorrow. Godly sorrow causes you to grieve over your sin, but it's a temporary thing. Once you've repented, godly sorrow is over and done with. In fact, God doesn't even remember your sin anymore and will never hold it over you. John says in 1 John 1:9 that **once you've repented and God forgives, you are proved innocent.** Let that word *innocent* rattle through your mind the next time Satan bombards you with his guilt attacks.

Refiner's Fire

Choosing to become a living sacrifice involves a total surrender to Jesus Christ. An essential part of that process is giving him permission to remove all of the buried sin in our lives and mold us into the kind of person he wants us to be. That's why the Old Testament book of Malachi refers to God as a "refiner's fire" (Mal. 3:2). This is a reference to the age-old process of purifying gold. When gold comes out of the ground, it is filled with impurities and isn't worth much. But a goldsmith takes that raw material and begins to mold a priceless treasure by putting the gold through a fiery furnace. The intense heat forces the dirt to rise to the molten surface, where it is swept away by the goldsmith. In the same way, when we surrender ourselves to God, he is going to refine and mold us in his refiner's fire so that we are purified and holy.

The problem is that Christians can become so entrapped in sin that they start to believe that God can't truly rescue them. If you struggle with that doubt, then you need to look again at the God of the Bible. As Caedmon's Call puts it in the second verse, God "stripped the trees of Lebanon." The "trees of Lebanon" are a symbol often used in the Bible (such as Ps. 104:16 and Isa. 14:8) to refer to the strongest trees of the ancient Near East. In a world before reinforced steel, concrete, and Kevlar, these trees were the toughest materials known to men. So if God is strong enough to handle the toughest the world has to offer, then he is certainly powerful enough to stomp out all of that buried sin in your life.

Some of the sin we need removed is obvious to us, particularly if it is something we do, act out, or participate in. But oftentimes the worst sins can actually be buried deep inside of us, hidden from other people. Caedmon's Call emphasizes two sins that can get masked in our hearts and that God must root out: false morality and selfish greed. The second verse continues,

You stripped the trees of Lebanon
And now you're stripping me
Of the bark of false morality
And the bite of selfish greed
Can you hear me

False morality is saying one thing and doing another. In other words, talking the talk but not walking the walk. It's becoming just like the Pharisees during the time of Jesus. To the everyday Jew, the Pharisees were the very definition of holiness. They were fanatics about not working on the Sabbath. They prayed visibly and vocally in public. And you would never find them in a sleazy bar, since they stayed away from any hint of visible sin.

Yet Jesus looked through their masks of false morality and saw them for who they really were—hypocrites. Underneath their masks were hearts empty of any real love for God.

While false morality makes us look good to people around us, selfish greed and pride can lurk underneath, filling our hearts with a constant desire for more, more, more. Caedmon's Call stresses the danger of this selfishness over other sins. False morality is the "bark," while selfish greed and pride are the "bite." If you've ever been around a rabid dog, you know the danger lies not in the bark but in the bite that follows it. And that selfishness, when left unchecked, will suffocate our faith and lead us into the same slavery that the prodigal son fell into.

Some Kind of Miracle

In the final verse of "Coming Home," Caedmon's Call uncovers the questions people face when they finally decide to turn back to God after their rebellion:

Will you run to me
Will you come to me
Will you meet me
Will you greet me
Will you drag me home
'Cause I'm still a long way off

When we begin to honestly understand the depth of sin in our lives, these kinds of questions are natural. As the prodigal son was walking on his long journey home, you can bet he was thinking the same thing. In the culture of the day, a son returning home after pulling such a stunt would have had to face a rough homecoming. Villagers would mock him relentlessly on his arrival, and his family would openly shame him. The prodigal would be forced to wait outside his father's house for a day or so before his father would agree to see him. After that, he could expect a severe beating. And if he was lucky enough to be able to stay, the best-case scenario he could hope for would be to stay on and work as a servant. The prodigal must have expected the worst, all the while hoping in the back of his mind for some kind of a miracle.

But whatever questions the prodigal had on his return journey, they were answered by the father through one amazing act. According to Luke 15:20, while the prodigal son "was still a long way off, his father saw him and was filled with compassion for him." The father's gut reaction was to sprint out to his son like an Olympian. He couldn't even wait for his son to return to the house!

The father's response may sound pretty amazing to us in the twenty-first century, but it was even more extraordinary to the people Jesus originally told the parable to. You see, in a culture where "saving face" could seem even as important as life itself, a father would never have reacted in that way—no matter what his feelings for his son. The father's action was humiliating enough, but the way in which he did it made it even worse. In the Middle Eastern culture of the day, no older man would *ever* run in public like that. To do so, he'd have to hold up his robe above his knees like a child and expose his undergarments as he ran. The whole spectacle would have been incredibly embarrassing for the father.

Can you see what the father did? He took on the shame and humiliation that the son should have received for himself. And, in case the parallel isn't obvious yet, that's exactly what Jesus did for you and me. Jesus Christ took on the shame of our sin and humiliated himself by dying on the cross.

But the father doesn't stop there. When he gets to his son, he showers him with love, throwing his arms around him and kissing him repeatedly. That's the picture Jesus was trying to paint of God's love for a world of prodigals. Therefore, the question "Will you run to me?" raised in "Coming Home" is answered by Jesus in a loud and clear voice: *Yes!* He will run to you, forgive you, and love you. You need just make the decision to come home to Jesus Christ.

★ ★ ★ **diving deeper** ★ ★ ★
Read Malachi 3:2; Luke 15;
Romans 12:1-2; 7:21-25; and 1 John 1:9.

The Christian Walk

COMING HOME
by Caedmon's Call

You say you want a living sacrifice
Well I am a burnt offering
Crawling off the altar and
Back into the fire

And with my smoke-filled lungs
I cry out for freedom
While locking and chaining myself
To my rotting desires

And I hate the stench
But I swallow the key
And with it stuck in my throat
Can you hear me

I'm coming home, I'm coming home
I'm coming home, I'm coming home
But I'm still a long way off

I am shelled-shocked and I have walked
Through the trenches full of tears
With the mortars of memory
Exploding in my burning ears

You stripped the trees of Lebanon
And now you're stripping me
Of the bark of false morality
And the bite of selfish greed
Can you hear me

I'm coming home, I'm coming home
I'm coming home, I'm coming home
But I'm still a long way off

Will you run to me
Will you come to me
Will you meet me
Will you greet me
Will you drag me home
'Cause I'm still a long way off

I'm coming home, I'm coming home
I'm coming home, I'm coming home
But I'm still a long way off

Used by permission. [16]

Action Steps

"Coming Home" focuses on the difficult and often painful struggle that overcoming sin can be in the life of a Christian. If sin has a hold on you, take the following steps:

- Be totally honest with yourself and identify the sin traps in your life that you have not been willing to give completely to God. Next, confess and repent of these sins, handing over these areas of your life to Jesus Christ.

- Commit yourself to living out Romans 12:1-2—being a living sacrifice, holy and pleasing to God.

- Be accountable to a friend in areas in which you are tempted. Meet with your friend regularly and commit to each other to be totally honest about your struggles.

- Set and stick to a consistent time for daily devotional reading and prayer to help you stay firmly grounded in the Bible rather than being reabsorbed into the world.

14

Spread-Eagled
Disciples

One doomsday scenario gives many people nightmares, but thankfully, few ever actually experience it in real life: imagine, for a moment, that you are trapped on the fourth floor of a burning skyscraper. Like a glutton devouring a five-course dinner, fire rips apart the building floor by floor, picking up speed as it moves to the floor you are on.

As you search desperately for an escape, you manage to find a windowed office untouched by the hungry flames. But as you pry open the window and look around, your hopes fade. The street seems impossibly far below. The firefighters looking up at you, however, have other ideas. You hear them screaming to jump, pointing to a safety net directly below your window.

Jump or not jump?

You would likely land safely, but the act of intentionally leaping out of a tall building goes against every urge inside of you. During the free fall, you would be completely helpless, dependent entirely on the safety net doing what it is supposed to do. If you were to go through with it, every ounce of strength you could muster would be required to take that final step into nothingness.

Real life is perhaps never as frantic as this desperate scenario, but we still face decisions that in their own way can seem every bit as scary and intimidating as this "jump or not jump" decision. In "Frail," Jars of Clay deals with one such issue in the life of a disciple—the decision to be broken before God. Through these lyrics, Jars of Clay reveals that being vulnerable for God is not something for cowards or the weak-hearted. Instead, brokenness requires a gutsy trust that God is going to catch you when you live fully for him.

We still face decisions that . . . seem every bit as scary . . . as this "jump or not jump" decision.

The Christian Walk

FUD

Frail. Just the word conjures up the image of a ninety-year-old woman in a nursing home or a newborn crying in his mother's arms. On first take, no word seems less descriptive of a Christian than being "frail." We usually hear upbeat Christian lingo like "Spirit-filled," "empowered," and "victorious" flow from church pulpits and best-selling Christian books. After all, since Jesus conquered death and gave Christians the Holy Spirit, shouldn't the Christian life be described with glowing, positive-sounding words?

But when we look at what Jesus calls his followers to do if they want to follow him, we discover that Christianity is all about being broken. Jesus broke his body on the cross. Paul talked of being poured out like a drink offering. In spite of the people they reached for Christ, Stephen and nearly all of the apostles died martyrs' deaths. In fact, after thumbing through the New Testament, one might even argue that "frailty" is the best term to describe Christian discipleship.

Jesus calls us to be broken so that he can accomplish his purposes in our life. In fact, only when we allow ourselves to become vulnerable does God reveal his power through us. Or, as 2 Corinthians 12:9–10 puts it, God's power is made perfect through our weaknesses. When we are weak, then we are strong.

Gideon, whose story is found in the book of Judges, is a great example of how God does great things through weakness. Gideon was a nobody—his family was part of the weakest clan in Israel, and he was the runt of his family. Yet God choose this most unlikely of people to lead the Israelite army to victory over their far more powerful enemy, the Midianites. When faced with this challenge, Gideon asked God, "Why me?" God's response was simply, "I will be with you" (Judg. 6:16). In other words, when God calls you to go out on a limb, he follows up that request with a promise to be with you in the midst of the hard times that follow.

Being frail is something that we can easily give lip service to, but when it comes down to actually doing it, we realize that brokenness is just plain hard. Satan and hesitation conspire against us. The world of marketing uses the term *FUD*, which is short for Fear, Uncertainty, and Doubt. Some companies use the cutthroat technique of FUD to get people to buy their products by trashing the integrity or reliability of their competitors. In the same way, Satan uses FUD as a way to muddy the waters, to prevent us from taking that final step to submission. As "Frail" begins, the opening lines focus on these kinds of doubts and fears that Satan loves to bring up:

> Convinced of my deception
> I've always been a fool
> I fear this love reaction
> Just like you said I would

Fear and self-doubt are great enemies of Christian disciples. They can cause us to shy away from the grace of God. After all, if you are convinced you are a "fool," then how can you be sure you know what truth is, much less actually live it out in your life? Defeatist expressions like "I'm a fool" and "I could never" easily creep into our vocabulary. The first verse of "Frail" continues, reinforcing these themes:

> A rose could never lie
> About the love it brings
> And I could never promise
> To be any of those things

The greatest of all flowers, the rose has been used by people for centuries as an expression of love for one another. It's an image of perfection, and something so perfect, in the words of the song, "could never lie." But when we have a poor self-image and start to compare ourselves to something flawless, we can begin to sink even further into a hole. We start to believe that we don't amount to anything. In our minds, other super-Christians may be able to live up to Jesus's call, but we could "never promise to be any of those things."

Excuses

Maybe they are excuses. Maybe they are explanations. But whatever we call them, they roll off our tongues as we explain why we cannot surrender and be broken. In the chorus of "Frail," Jars of Clay lists several of these reasons:

> If I was not so weak
> If I was not so cold
> If I was not so scared of being broken
> Growing old
> I would be
> I would be

In these lyrics, Jars of Clay highlights four main obstacles that can prevent Christians from becoming frail.

First, we can be too weak to become weak. Human weakness, the kind of weakness that Jars of Clay is singing about here, paralyzes us and forces us to cling to the security of the world. It is the opposite of the frailty that Jesus Christ displayed. **Christlike frailty is a spread-eagle jump,** abandoning all to

God; in contrast, human weakness resembles a fetal position curl as we shrink back from everyone.

Second, our hearts can become so cold and calloused that we become unwilling to surrender our lives to Christ. When we cling to the world for security and meaning, our disobedience will gradually produce a hardness in our hearts. We begin to care less and less about God and others around us. We become more absorbed in our own wants and needs. And we become desensitized to sin in our lives. When this coldness sets in, we start to lose conviction that we even need to be broken.

Third, we can become terrified at the prospect of being broken by God. No matter how much confidence we have in God's promises, brokenness is a scary thing. Every instinct we have screams out for self-preservation. Then, when we turn our eyes away from God and onto the circumstances of life, we can convince ourselves that God isn't really going to take care of us, that his safety net will give way under the weight of our problems. Brokenness becomes a death march, a walk we cannot make.

Fourth, we can become scared of losing what makes us strong and unique. When Jars of Clay sings, "If I was not so scared of . . . growing old," old age is signifying lost opportunities, becoming a "has-been." Frailty can become tainted with thoughts of giving up our youth and surrendering what makes us unique.

Exposed

When we are faced with the task of doing something unpleasant, the natural human impulse is to escape. If you have a killer final exam, you long for a blizzard to put off the unpleasantness for a little while longer. Need your wisdom teeth pulled? Your mind is already scheming to find some excuse to postpone your appointment until next month. Likewise, when we are confronted with the call of Jesus to be broken, our gut reaction may be to plug our ears and ignore the call. In the words of Jars of Clay, we try to find "some comfort in rooms I try to hide."

As the old saying goes, ignorance is bliss. In other words, sometimes the less we know, the happier we will be. That's the kind of plug-your-ears escape that Jars of Clay longs for in the second verse of "Frail":

Blessed are the shallow
Depth they'll never find
Seems to be some comfort
In rooms I try to hide

When God confronts us on an issue, our eyes can start to rove; we look at friends around us who seem to be doing just fine, thank you very much, relying on their own strength and abilities rather than abandoning themselves to Christ. Perhaps those friends are not as mature spiritually, but their shallowness looks quite appealing. We too would like to avoid the "depth they'll never find." However, God loves us too much to let us get away with escaping his call. We can run from God, but we can't hide. God is relentless when he calls us and will expose us as we attempt to hide in the shadows.

Brokenness becomes a death march, a walk we cannot make.

Another technique we may use to hide from all-out brokenness is placing conditions on our decision. We'll agree to jump, so to speak, but we want to tell the firefighters where to put the safety net or how high the net should be off of the ground. In his devotional *My Utmost for His Highest*, Oswald Chambers puts this issue into perspective:

> God can never make us wine if we object to the fingers He uses to crush us with. If God would only use His own fingers, and make me broken bread and poured-out wine in a special way! But when He uses someone whom we dislike, or some set of circumstances to which we said we would never submit, and makes those the crushers, we object. We must never choose the scene of our own martyrdom. If ever we are going to be made into wine, we will have to be crushed; you cannot drink grapes. Grapes become wine only when they have been squeezed.[1]

We can kick and scream as we approach the decision for brokenness, but Jars of Clay alludes to three blessings that come about in our lives when we take the plunge: freedom, healing, and peace. The lyrics put it like this:

> Exposed beyond the shadows
> You take the cup from me
> Your dirt removes my blindness
> Your pain becomes my peace

When we become broken for God, Jesus promises to "take the cup" from us. There's an incredible freedom that goes along with that promise. Though we may experience tough times and hardship when we are obedient, we are freed from worrying about the consequences. That's God's business.

We experience this freedom because Jesus already took the cup for himself. On the night before his crucifixion, Jesus prayed in the Garden of Gethsemane, asking his Father for a way out (Matt. 26:36–42). But because no other alternative would bring about salvation, Jesus willingly drank the cup of sin and death,

The Christian Walk

just so we don't have to. Therefore, when we join with him and become like broken bread and poured-out wine, Jesus promises that our sacrifice will not be as hard as we think. Or, as Jesus said: "My yoke is easy and my burden is light" (Matt. 11:30).

Jesus will also heal you spiritually and restore you emotionally when you commit to him. John 9 tells the story of Jesus healing a blind man by spitting on the ground, making some mud with the saliva, and rubbing the dirt on the man's eyes. In the same way, his "dirt" will spiritually heal us as we give over our lives to him.

Finally, when we are broken, Jesus will give us peace that is beyond our wildest dreams. The Bible calls it "peace . . . which surpasses all understanding" (Phil. 4:7 NKJV). That peace is possible because of the suffering that Jesus endured on the cross. Because of his pain, Jesus conquered death. The result for us is peace, even in the midst of the most awful doomsday scenarios we may encounter in life.

In this part of "Frail," Jars of Clay also underscores the fact that Christianity is not a self-help religion. Freedom, healing, and peace aren't found by being a nice person or doing good works for God. Instead, as the lyrics show, Jesus is the person making these promises possible: "You take the cup from me / Your dirt removes my blindness / Your pain becomes my peace." Jesus is the active party; we simply respond by taking the leap.

Last Moments

While the theme of the song is brokenness, the word *frail* is carefully avoided until the last possible moment. The first time the chorus is sung, for example, the line "I would be" is repeated two times, but the thought is never finished. Instead, it is not until the final chorus that the singer is able to gather enough courage to utter that word. The reason for the delay in delivering that final line is crystal clear: we will wait until the last possible moment to become broken and surrender everything to Jesus.

Have you made a commitment to Jesus to become broken for him? Don't look around for alternatives, see whether your friends are doing it, or put off the decision until a later time. Instead, make the spread-eagle jump today and experience the freedom, healing, and peace that you can only find by being frail.

★ ★ ★ diving deeper ★ ★ ★

Read Judges 6:11–16; Micah 7:8; Luke 22:39–42; John 9:1–11; 2 Corinthians 12:9–10; 13:3–4; Philippians 2:17.

Read *The Cost of Discipleship* by Dietrich Bonhoeffer. It is a challenging book but worth the effort if you stick with it. Read *My Utmost for His Highest* by Oswald Chambers, a daily devotional that will continually remind you to become a "spread-eagled disciple."

Read *Oswald Chambers: Abandoned to God* by David McCasland to learn about a man who spent his life "free falling" for God.

FRAIL
by Jars of Clay

Convinced of my deception
I've always been a fool
I fear this love reaction
Just like you said I would
A rose could never lie
About the love it brings
And I could never promise
To be any of those things

[Chorus:]
If I was not so weak
If I was not so cold
If I was not so scared of being broken
Growing old
I would be
I would be

Blessed are the shallow
Depth they'll never find
Seems to be some comfort
In rooms I try to hide
Exposed beyond the shadows
You take the cup from me
Your dirt removes my blindness
Your pain becomes my peace

[Chorus]

I would be
I would be
Frail

Used by permission. [17]

Action Steps

The song "Frail" becomes a confession that exposes the struggle that Christians can have over being broken for Jesus Christ. If you struggle with brokenness as the song depicts, take the following steps toward frailty:

- Fear of the unknown turns many disciples into Christian cowards. Look into a mirror and see if you can see this fear in your eyes. If so, ask God for the courage to jump.
- Take the first step. Tell God you are willing to be broken for him and look for practical ways to live out that commitment. Don't make being frail harder than it really is. Brokenness is not a matter of human effort; it is a decision to be vulnerable for God. Therefore, responding to God's call is simply a matter of risking that first step.
- When you become broken for God, do not get picky and start telling God how to use you. You cannot place conditions on your brokenness; it is an all-or-nothing proposition.
- Pick up a copy of Oswald Chambers's My Utmost for His Highest and commit to reading the devotional each morning. Chambers will teach you much about becoming broken for Jesus Christ.

15

Thrill
Seekers

In our so often sanitized and predictable society, many have made thrill seeking a way of life, even an obsession. There's heli-skiing in British Columbia. Parasailing in Florida. Cliff diving in Hawaii. Mountain climbing in the Himalayas. And for those who can't afford those exotic locales, there are the thrillers for the rest of us—roller coasters at Six Flags and virtual-reality rides at Disney World. No matter where we go, we can shell out a wad of bucks and experience excitement that we will rave about—at least until the next adventure comes along. But the problem with today's thrills is that they soon become a "been there, done that." They never satisfy. **The rush is never quite the same the second and third time around.** So people move on, continuing on an endless search for more excitement.

This desire for seeking thrills is natural; it's part of how God made us. God never intended for us to live lives of boredom and timidity. No, he created us for exciting stuff. But we won't find his thrills on a parachute jump or a corkscrew coaster. These are cheap substitutes for God's idea of an adrenaline rush. According to the Bible, real thrill seeking is found in the most unlikely of places: the everyday life of an obedient disciple.

Steven Curtis Chapman in his song "Dive" and the Newsboys in "Deep End" sing about the adventure God has prepared for each Christian. Through these songs, they challenge us to take the ultimate thrill ride—living as a disciple of Jesus Christ.

Each Christian experiences an unavoidable face-to-face.

Living in the Rapids

Each Christian experiences an unavoidable face-to-face. At some point, Jesus Christ is going to meet us at a cliff's edge. He will stop us where we are and ask us to choose whether we are going to jump off—live sold out for him—or are going to stay put on solid ground. During his ministry on earth, Jesus brought people to this ledge all of the time. In Matthew 8:18–22, two men came to Jesus and said that they wanted to follow him. As pleased as Jesus was by their offers, he wanted them to fully understand what they were getting into. So he told them flat out that following him meant leaving behind all that they held dear—take it or leave it. Similarly, the rich ruler in Luke 18 "talked the talk," but Jesus saw through all the nice-sounding words. Jesus brought the young man to that cliff's edge, forcing him to choose between his money and his God.

As "Dive" begins, Steven Curtis Chapman sings about how Christ inevitably will bring us to this same decision point:

The long awaited rains
Have fallen hard upon the thirsty ground
And carved their way to where
The wild and rushing river can be found
And like the rains
I have been carried here to where the river
    flows, yeah

When "long awaited rains have fallen hard upon the thirsty ground," they naturally "carve their way" in the direction of a "wild and rushing river." If you have ever tried to divert rain from its natural path to another location, you know exactly how difficult it is to stop the water's natural flow. Just as the course of rainwater into the river is unavoidable, so too is Christ's call for us. When Jesus brings us to that decision point, we will no longer be able to get away with cramming our faith into Sunday mornings. Faith becomes something we have to live out 24/7.

When Jesus takes us to the edge of the cliff, he may ask us to go do something that doesn't make sense from the world's perspective. Maybe he will call you to serve as a missionary in a war-torn country. To work in a job that doesn't pay nearly enough to survive on. To delay your career or schooling altogether so you can serve someone around you in need. To take an unpopular stand among your friends at work or school.

As Chapman continues in the first verse, he describes this moment in which we have to decide whether to jump or not:

My heart is racing and my knees are weak
As I walk to the edge
I know there is no turning back
Once my feet have left the ledge
And in the rush I hear a voice
That's telling me it's time to take the leap of faith
So here I go

When we reach that decision point, we can feel the same queasy feeling in our stomachs as if we were actually on top of a mountain looking down onto a valley hundreds of feet below. We realize that once we jump off, there is no turning back.

Using similar imagery in "Deep End," the Newsboys start off their song by singing about a girl who has made this same decision to jump off into the water:

She's diving down
Gonna make her home now
The ocean
She's done with living her life
On the ground
She's sinking down
Hands above her
Held her
Nineteen years
And now they're letting go

This girl finally realized that she couldn't have an authentic faith living in two worlds, though she tried for nineteen years. Seeing the waste of a lukewarm life, she's "gonna make her home now / the ocean / she's done with living her life / on the ground." We all have to get to this same point of being ready to let our hands go.

This act of jumping off, however, is a scary business. But as Chapman sings in the chorus of "Dive," when we do so, we experience the ultimate adventure, far better than parasailing or skydiving could ever be. The lyrics go:

I'm diving in, I'm going deep, in over my
   head, I want to be
Caught in the rush, lost in the flow, in over my
   head, I want to go

The river's deep, the river's wide, the river's
water is alive
So sink or swim, I'm diving in

What an incredible ride a life of faith is! Never mistake discipleship as a summer swim in a serene lake. No, it is a thrill ride down Class 5 rapids with danger lurking around every corner. The peril comes when we release our hands before we know how it is all going to turn out. We leave the safety net of the world and our own strength, and we "sink or swim" based solely on God's help. Yet because of this potential danger, life as a disciple is also exhilarating when we watch God working all around us. He will fill our lives with the same risk-taking thrills that we previously sought in amusement parks or on the ski slopes.

Yet the Newsboys warn about the problems we can expect as we swim through these rapids:

She's going off
The deep end
Breaking from the crowd
She's way in over her head
I think she's gonna drown

People, even other Christians, may doubt our decision and think we are "going off the deep end." When we are "breaking from the crowd," we go against common sense, what is normal, what is expected of us. Even our friends and family can think we are "way over [our] head" and be convinced we are "gonna drown." Sometimes that pressure to be just like everyone else or live up to other people's expectations is hard to deal with. We

Give your worry to Jesus
Christ and stand back in
wonder.

can start to question ourselves and wonder if we misread God's will all along.

What's more, we can simply get intimidated by our dangerous surroundings, even when we think we are trusting God fully and know the promises of the Bible by heart. When we see the rapids around us, our imaginations can run wild and get carried away with doomsday scenarios. C. S. Lewis wrote, "We can face things which we know to be dangerous; our real trouble is often with things we know to be safe but which look dreadful."[1] What Lewis meant is that we so easily get caught up with how bleak our circumstances appear to be. We forget that God is involved and in control over all things.

The Newsboys challenge us, when faced with this doubt and questioning, to take the plunge without worry and stress. In the bridge of "Deep End," they sing:

> To take this step of faith
> Don't need to be scared
> Turn worry into wonder
> Dissolve the fear

Don't waste your time dwelling on the worst-case scenarios and scheming up ways to free yourself from them. Oswald Chambers believed that the "one great crime" of Christians is worry. "Whenever we begin to calculate without God," explained Chambers, "we commit sin."[2] Instead, we are to do as the Newsboys sing: "turn worry into wonder / dissolve the fear." Give your worry to Jesus Christ and stand back in wonder as he works a mighty miracle in your situation.

As the Newsboys remind us in "Deep End," when we dive in, "tomorrow will be 'round / and everyone will see / no tragedy." We can fear the unknown and circumstances that look scary, but

God is not going to abandon us. In fact, the only real tragedy is the Christian left behind, frozen on solid ground, too scared to jump off in obedience.

What New Life Brings

As Steven Curtis Chapman continues in the second verse of "Dive," he sings of the power that is unleashed in the life of a disciple who makes this risky decision:

> There is a supernatural power
> In this mighty river's flow
> It can bring the dead to life
> And it can fill an empty soul
> And give a heart the only thing
> Worth living and worth dying for, yeah

When we jump in, we are going to be swimming in the "supernatural power in this mighty river's flow." According to Chapman, God's power produces three things in our lives.

First, when we dive in, God gives us a life of adventure. We know by thumbing through the Bible that God's power can quite literally "bring the dead to life." But Jesus Christ does not simply pump a pulse through your veins; he also transforms a dull, boring, and calculating life into a life of thrill seeking. "Life is not a problem to be solved," says author John Eldredge. "It is an adventure to be lived."[3] Eldredge is exactly right; God wants us to do far more than just survive. We'll find no greater thrill than living on the edge for Jesus Christ. We may be asked to risk our career, our relationships, our finances, and even our physical safety. But when we do so, God releases his supernatural power through us, empowering us to meet the difficult challenges that await us.

Second, diving in gives us hope. The name of the secular alternative band Smile Empty Soul symbolizes the world's useless struggle for any lasting hope—making the best of an otherwise meaningless existence. But, as Chapman sings, God longs to "fill an empty soul," not cover it over with fake smiles. So when we dive in, he fills us with the hope we are seeking. We no longer have to go through the motions of life doing what others expect of us. Instead, we can have the hope that Jesus Christ is in control and will work wonders in our lives.

Third, when we dive in, God supplies us with a purpose. When we live sold out for Christ, God gives us, in the words of Chapman, "the only thing worth living and worth dying for." God gives us a purpose in life, a reason to live. We will be spending our energies on things that have eternal significance and value.

But we never get to know God's life, hope, and purpose when we sit idly by on solid ground and take comfort in the firm footing of the world. Chapman reminds us that we "will never know the awesome power of the grace of God until we let ourselves get swept away into this holy flood."

Really Believing

Tightrope walking has always been a thrill that spectators line up to see. Perhaps the most famous tightrope walker of all was a man known as the Great Blondin, back in the nineteenth century. One day he was performing for a large crowd, attempting to cross a tightrope strung across the Niagara River, not far from Niagara Falls. Before beginning the stunt, he teased the crowd, "Do you believe that the Great Blondin can make it across this mighty river on this tiny tightrope?"

The crowd screamed back, "Yes! You can do it. We know you can!"

So Blondin began his journey to the other side of the river and then back again, as cheers encouraged him all along the way. After finishing the first stunt, Blondin put a wheelbarrow on the tightrope and asked the excited crowd, "Do you believe I can push this wheelbarrow back and forth across the tightrope?"

"Yes!" cried the people.

Blondin took it a step further. "Okay, do you believe I can do it with someone riding in the wheelbarrow?"

The crowd yelled, "We believe! We believe!"

Then Blondin zinged the crowd, "So who among you is going to be that person to ride along?"

Upon hearing this challenge, the crowd fell deathly silent.

Like the crowd watching Blondin, we easily say we believe. We find it easy to get pumped up with stories of other Christians diving in, risking everything for Christ, while we remain on the safety of solid ground. But when Jesus takes us to that cliff's edge and the questions start to get personal, then there's no hiding among the crowd.

Steven Curtis Chapman closes "Dive" with this challenge:

So if you'll take my hand
We'll close our eyes and count to three
And take the leap of faith
Come on let's go

Don't let yourself stay as one of crowd watching Blondin. Instead, go to that cliff's edge, close your eyes, count to three, and take the leap of faith. Come on, let's go!

DIVE
by Steven Curtis Chapman

The long awaited rains
Have fallen hard upon the thirsty ground
And carved their way to where
The wild and rushing river can be found
And like the rains
I have been carried here to where the river
  flows, yeah
My heart is racing and my knees are weak
As I walk to the edge
I know there is no turning back
Once my feet have left the ledge
And in the rush I hear a voice
That's telling me it's time to take the leap
  of faith
So here I go

I'm diving in, I'm going deep, in over my
  head, I want to be
Caught in the rush, lost in the flow, in over
  my head, I want to go

The river's deep, the river's wide, the
  river's water is alive
So sink or swim, I'm diving in

There is a supernatural power
In this mighty river's flow
It can bring the dead to life
And it can fill an empty soul
And give a heart the only thing
Worth living and worth dying for, yeah
But we will never know the awesome
  power
Of the grace of God
Until we let ourselves get swept away
Into this holy flood
So if you'll take my hand
We'll close our eyes and count to three
And take the leap of faith
Come on let's go

DEEP END
by the Newsboys

She's diving down
Gonna make her home now
The ocean
She's done with living her life
On the ground
She's sinking down
Hands above her
Held her
Nineteen years
And now they're letting go
Tomorrow will be 'round
And everyone will see
No tragedy
It's like it's over
But it's just begun

She's going off
The deep end
Breaking from the crowd
She's way over her head
I think she's gonna drown
She's going off
The deep end
The search is over now
She's falling into your hands
It's all or nothing
There's no guessing
She's been lost and found

She's diving down
Scars on her elbows
The wind blows
An old song spins around inside
"How sweet the sound"
To be living
And dying
Looks like it's over
But it's just begun

To take this step of faith
Don't need to be scared
Turn worry into wonder
Dissolve the fear
She's steppin' out
And you drop the blame
As she speaks the name
Above all other names

To be lost and found
Her world has turned
Upside down
Her soul restored
With salt like rain
From all of the things
That you forgave
And all the times she'd disobey
She's diving in the ocean of your grace

Action Steps

Both Steven Curtis Chapman in "Dive" and the Newsboys in "Deep End" sing about the leap of faith that Jesus asks of every person who wants to be his disciple. As you look at your life of faith, actively take the following actions:

Take ten minutes to examine the areas of your life that you are too scared to trust to God. Then prayerfully meet Jesus Christ at the cliff's edge and take the leap of faith by asking him to take control of those areas.

Walk wisely. Don't go looking for risk for the sake of risk itself. But when God is clearly calling you, don't hesitate to dive into situations that look scary and intimidating

Read a biography of missionary Hudson Taylor to see firsthand how he lived sold out for Jesus Christ on a daily basis.

★★★ diving deeper ★★★
Read Matthew 8:18-22 and Luke 18:18-29.

Christian Walk

16

The Icarus Confession

"I can fly!" Icarus shouted with delight as he gazed upon the glimmering Mediterranean Sea below him. With his hands clasping a homemade pair of wings, Icarus was starting to feel invincible. The island of Crete, which moments before had been his prison, now resembled a small pebble, ready to be skipped across the open sea that surrounded it.

"With these wings, there's nothing I can't do, no place I can't explore," Icarus trumpeted as he inched ever higher in the sky.

The wings held by Icarus were built by his father, Daedalus, so the twosome could escape captivity. He had constructed the wings from wood and feathers and bonded them together with wax. Daedalus had equipped himself with a set and given the other to his son with a strict warning not to fly too near the sun or the wax would melt.

But as he soared thousands of feet in the air, Icarus was having too much fun to heed his father's advice. Anything now seemed possible, and Icarus pushed ever upward to see his newfound playground. Although Icarus paid no notice, the heat from the sun became more and more intense. Slowly the wax fixing the feathers onto the wooden frame began to bubble.

Flying far below, Daedalus watched in horror as his son's wings started disintegrating before his eyes. He shouted for Icarus to come lower, but Icarus was far too preoccupied with his success to hear his father. Moments later, when most of the feathers had fallen away, Icarus was jolted

Once we let our pride control us . . . we'll eventually fly "too high" as we move away from God.

from his dreams as he realized the wings could no longer hold him up. Madly flapping the wooden frames, Icarus made a frantic attempt to save himself. But gravity soon won. Icarus plunged to his death in the sea that just moments before was the floor to his vast playground.

Despite being thousands of years old, the Greek myth of Icarus is as useful today as ever in showing the dangers of human pride. Indeed, the story of Icarus's disastrous flight serves as the starting point for Jars of Clay's "Worlds Apart" as it explores what happens when pride invades our spiritual lives. Through this song, Jars of Clay gives a deeply personal account of a struggle that all believers face: how to faithfully live as a disciple in a sinful world without crashing and burning like Icarus did.

Battlegrounds of Pride

"Worlds Apart" starts off with a "slap in the face" truth that you and I and every other Christian must deal with:

> I am the only one to blame for this
> Somehow it all adds up the same
> Soaring on the wings of selfish pride
> I flew too high and like Icarus I collide
> With a world I try so hard to leave behind

These opening lines expose the most dangerous sin that can dog our life of faith: selfish pride. Pride not only causes us to become absorbed with ourselves and our happiness but also triggers other sins such as lying, stealing, or cheating. Once we let our pride control us, we'll soar for a while like Icarus, but, as the song says, we'll eventually fly "too high" as we move away from God.

"When a man comes to Jesus," Oswald Chambers said, "it is not sin that is in the way, but his claim to himself."[1] When we make the decision to become a Christian and accept Jesus Christ as our Savior, we are admitting that we can't save ourselves on our own. But because of deep-rooted selfishness, we'll still have a claim to our lives and yearn to live them the way we want to. Battle lines are then drawn inside our hearts and minds: grace on one side, pride on the other. In "Worlds Apart," Jars of Clay uncovers this "battle between grace and pride." Fights are constantly being waged between Christ living in us and our dying sin nature that is hell-bent on not losing control.

Sometimes we may not even realize this battle is taking place inside of us. **We can try really hard to live for Christ but still become absorbed with our hopes, our accomplishments, and our future.** Even the desire to "make a difference" can sometimes be nothing more than something that *we* want to accomplish for God rather than a sincere desire to live out our faith.

When we are "soaring on the wings of selfish pride," we'll also try to live the Christian life on our own strength and resolve rather than relying on Christ. It's easy to keep busy doing Christian stuff—going to a Bible study, talking about our faith with friends, or volunteering at church—all the while letting our prayer and devotional time slip as a lower and lower priority in our days. With a focus on *doing* things for God rather than *being* with him, we become his servant in name only and have little relationship with him personally. The end result: we become just like Icarus as we soar higher and higher in the sky. For a while we can fool ourselves, but sooner or later our self-made contraption will come crashing down on top of us.

All-Out Obedience

In "Worlds Apart," Jars of Clay makes it clear that Jesus is not satisfied with this kind of self-absorbed, self-reliant faith. He wants more from those who follow him. The first verse of the song speaks to this point when it cries out for change:

To rid myself of all but love
To give and die

Everyone who wants to follow Christ must do the same thing—rid themselves "of all but love" and "give and die." These lyrics remind us of Mark 8:34. In this verse Jesus says, "If anyone would come after me, he must deny himself and take up his cross and follow me." He adds in Matthew 10:39, "Whoever loses his life for my sake will find it." When we read these passages, we may try to treat Jesus's commands with kid gloves, writing them off as the exaggerated lines of a coach's speech before a big game. We rationalize, *He doesn't intend that I take his command literally, right?* But Dietrich Bonhoeffer, who was a pastor martyred in Nazi Germany, put Jesus's command in crystal-clear terms when he said, "When Christ calls a man he bids him 'come and die.'"[2] In other words, Jesus Christ says that if you are going to follow him, he wants every part of you. One hundred percent. Shedding everything else and being totally loyal to him. That's what "dying to self" means.

Jesus asks all-out obedience from us for a very practical reason: only the person who is dead to his or her own will is able to truly follow him. But in practice, giving your will to Jesus is harder than it sounds. Oh, it is natural to be single-minded and enthusiastic about something. When we get distracted by the world around us, we can easily become absorbed with material things, status, or simply having a good time. Even when we mature in our faith and overcome some of those worldly traps, we are still not out of the woods; we can actually find ourselves becoming more committed to a cause, a calling, or a ministry than to Christ himself.

Jesus didn't call just a handful of people two thousand years ago to be his disciples. Jesus calls *every* Christian to follow him. The only question is how each of us is going to answer back. As "Worlds Apart" illustrates, "self" can easily get in the way of all-out obedience, causing us to accept discipleship on *our* terms rather than on his.

A Struggling Faith

Our selfish nature not only tempts us to disregard Jesus's call to make him Master of our lives, but when we mix pride together with a struggling, incomplete faith, we can begin to lose sight of our need for Christ as our Savior as well. The second verse of "Worlds Apart" deals with this struggle, trying to make sense of what Christ did:

All said and done I stand alone
Amongst remains of a life I should not own
It takes all I am to believe
In the mercy that covers me
Did you really have to die for me?
All I am for all you are
Because what I need and what I believe are
   worlds apart

We so easily take God's grace for granted. We start to minimize our sin, rationalize our behavior, and fool ourselves into believing that maybe we're not so bad after all. When this happens, as the song says, we begin to question God and ask, "Did you *really* have to die for me?" "Worlds Apart" comes back to this problem once again at the opening of its extended final verse:

I look beyond the empty cross
Forgetting what my life has cost
So wipe away the crimson stains
And dull the nails that still remain

When we "look beyond the empty cross," "wipe away the crimson stains," and "dull the nails that still remain," we are transforming God's costly gift of grace into a bargain basement substitute that trivializes the cross and even Jesus Christ.

Either/Or

"Worlds Apart" wakes us up from the fantasyland that our pride and weak faith can build around us by talking about sin in very graphic terms. Taking us to the scene of Jesus dying on the cross, Jars of Clay says that when we go our own way, we are actually participating in this crucifixion. As the song describes, our sin becomes "another nail to pierce the skin" of Jesus. Jars of Clay then continues by asking us to consider this question:

Can I be the one to sacrifice
Or grip the spear and watch the blood and
water flow

These lines drive home the point that if we are not willing to live all out for Christ, we are not just lukewarm Christians—we are just like the Roman soldier who took a spear and plunged it through Christ's body as he hung on the cross (John 19:34). Considering what Jars of Clay means by this, we can see that living the life of a disciple boils down to a single decision: *will you crucify Christ or be crucified with Christ?* There's no third, more pleasant alternative available for us to choose. It's an either/or decision.

If we don't want to join in crucifying Christ, our only choice is to come alongside Jesus at the cross, to die along with him and become a suffering servant. For God is a God who suffers, Bonhoeffer wrote. Jesus took on human flesh, endured the cross, and suffered for our sin. In the same way, we are also called upon to sacrifice and endure. According to Bonhoeffer, that is exactly what it means to be a Christian.

Turning the Corner

When we are honest with ourselves and begin to see our sin as God sees it, we finally begin to understand that we can't live the Christian life on our own strength. We need God's help!

"Worlds Apart" reminds us of two steps we must take to produce lasting change in our walk with Christ: accepting responsibility for our own actions and inviting Jesus to shake our world and tear it apart.

First, when we stumble and fall, we can easily be tempted to make excuses, rationalize our actions in light of circumstances, or fault others, even God. Yet nowhere in "Worlds Apart" is anyone else held responsible. In the very first line of the song, Jars of Clay makes it clear that blame is placed squarely on our shoulders alone when they sing, "I am the only one to blame for this." This confession at the beginning sets the stage for real change later in the song. That's

Will you crucify Christ or be crucified with Christ?

The Christian Walk

because when we become aware of our sin and selfishness and repent of it, the Holy Spirit, who lives inside every believer, can start the process of molding our hearts and shaping us as he wants to. Accepting responsibility for our sins isn't enough by itself, but it's the starting point for allowing God to transform us.

Second, "Worlds Apart" is at its heart an open invitation to Jesus Christ to shake our world from its foundations. The song's chorus repeats this request:

> To love you—take my world apart
> To need you—I am on my knees
> To love you—take my world apart
> To need you—broken on my knees

The chorus illustrates that the way we can show love toward God is by allowing him to take our worlds apart. And once we fully realize how much we need him to take control over our lives, we'll end up "broken" on our knees.

Jars of Clay returns to this theme in the concluding lines of the song. As the driving acoustic guitar reaches a peak, each line seems to build on the next, inviting Christ to take our worlds apart:

> So steal my heart and take the pain
> And wash the feet and cleanse my pride
> Take the selfish, take the weak,
> And all the things I cannot hide
> Take the beauty, take my tears
> The sin-soaked heart and make it yours
> Take my world all apart
> Take it now, take it now
> And serve the ones that I despise

Speak the words I can't deny
Watch the world I used to love
Fall to dust and thrown away

Dying to self involves giving Christ all parts of our lives—the good, the bad, and the ugly. We need to allow him to get rid of all of the crud that we cannot hide in our sin-soaked hearts. We also need to give away our agendas and deep-seated desires to find security in the world rather than in him. Finally, we need to lay before Jesus our service, talents, beauty, and tears so that he can use them for what he wants, not what we want.

Becoming More of Yourself

All this talk of "dying to self" might sound like the Christian life is one of hardship, strict rules, and giving up everything that makes us happy. But in reality, the opposite is the case. When we allow Jesus to take our worlds apart, he doesn't just swallow up all of the good stuff and leave us empty-handed. Instead, he fills us with so much more than we could ever have on our own. C. S. Lewis pointed out this truth when he wrote:

> [God] wants to detach men from themselves. When [God] talks of their losing their selves, he only means abandoning the clamor of self-will; once they have done that, he really gives them back all their personality, and boasts that when they are wholly his they will be more themselves than ever.[3]

The great surprise of the Christian life is that when we die to ourselves and go all out in obedience and loyalty to Christ, we will actually become *more* of ourselves, more of who we truly are created to be, than if we go our own Icarus-like way. In "Worlds Apart," Jars of Clay shows us the narrow road to get there.

WORLDS APART
by Jars of Clay

I am the only one to blame for this
Somehow it all adds up the same
Soaring on the wings of selfish pride
I flew too high and like Icarus I collide
With a world I try so hard to leave behind
To rid myself of all but love, to give and die
To turn away and not become
Another nail to pierce the skin of one who
    loves

More deeply than the oceans
More abundant than the tear
Of a world embracing every heartache
Can I be the one to sacrifice
Or grip the spear and watch the blood and
    water flow

[Chorus:]
To love you— take my world apart
To need you— I am on my knees
To love you—take my world apart
To need you—broken on my knees

All said and done I stand alone
Amongst remains of a life I should not own
It takes all I am to believe
In the mercy that covers me
Did you really have to die for me?
All I am for all you are
Because what I need and what I believe are
    worlds apart

[Chorus]

I look beyond the empty cross
Forgetting what my life has cost
And wipe away the crimson stains
And dull the nails that still remain
More and more I need you now,
I owe you more each passing hour
The battle between grace and pride
I gave up not so long ago
So steal my heart and take the pain
And wash the feet and cleanse my pride
Take the selfish, take the weak,
And all the things I cannot hide
Take the beauty, take my tears
The sin-soaked heart and make it yours
Take my world all apart
Take it now, take it now

And serve the ones that I despise
Speak the words I can't deny
Watch the world I used to love
Fall to dust and thrown away
I look beyond the empty cross
Forgetting what my life has cost
So wipe away the crimson stains
And dull the nails that still remain
So steal my heart and take the pain
Take the selfish, take the weak
And all the things I cannot hide
Take the beauty, take my tears
Take my world apart, take my world apart
I pray, I pray, I pray
Take my world apart

Action Steps

The title "Worlds Apart" has a double meaning. First, it is a confession that so often where you are as a disciple is worlds apart from where you should be. Second, the title serves as an invitation to God to take your world apart, to make you die to yourself and become a suffering servant just like Christ was.

If you'd like to invite God to take your world apart, pray and act upon each of the following steps:

Carve out an entire afternoon from your normal life to get alone with God. When you do so, do the following steps:

- recognize the selfish pride in your life
- accept responsibility for your sin
- make the decision to be a suffering servant who is crucified with Christ
- ask God to take your world apart and put it back in the way he wants to

Spend time with God daily in prayer and Bible reading to fight the natural tendency to try to live the Christian life on your own strength.

Read at least the first five chapters of The Cost of Discipleship by Dietrich Bonhoeffer. It's a challenging book but one that will deepen your Christian walk as you work through it, particularly chapters 1–5.

★★★ **diving deeper** ★★★

Read Matthew 10:38–39; Mark 8:34; Luke 5:27–28;
14:27; 18:18–23; Galatians 2:20.

Read *The Cost of Discipleship* by Dietrich Bonhoeffer.

Part Five

Living
in the
W

Every generation of Christians faces unique challenges. . . . The challenge of living with popular culture may well be as serious for modern Christians as persecution and plagues were for the saints of earlier centuries.

Kenneth A. Myers,
All God's Children and Blue Suede Shoes

*What's it gonna take
to slow us down
to let the silence spin us around?*
    Switchfoot, "Adding to the Noise"

orld

17

Out of Your
Comfort
Zone

Comfy. That's the adjective that describes much of the Christian church today. Many of us live in suburban neighborhoods, attend well-furnished churches, and go off to work or school for a few hours before returning to our comfy homes. Our lives seep with all things Christian: we have Christian music to jam to, Christian books to read, Christian bookstores to shop at, and Christian magazines to subscribe to. We lead busy lives but try our best to carve out time each day to be alone with God. In reading Jesus's command to "love your neighbor as yourself," we feel satisfied. After all, we try hard to be friendly to people and would certainly help a neighbor out in a crunch. Yet as we live 24/7 in this comfortable Christian mini-world all our own, we create an unintended side effect: we are building up walls between us and the world outside our doors. As a result, much of the church has become irrelevant to and out of touch with people most in need.

much of the church has become irrelevant to and out of touch with people most in need.

Point of Grace wants to shake us out of our comfy little worlds. With that goal in mind, they sing in "Saving Grace" about the responsibility that each Christian has to reach out to a lost and desperate world.

Throwaways

In "Saving Grace," Point of Grace sings about a fifteen-year-old girl who grew up in a single-parent family. Since Grace's father "left home before she arrived," life for Grace and her mother is tough, "just getting by on their own." Eventually things get so bad that Grace runs away. But whatever hopes and dreams she may have had in leaving are quickly dashed by the harsh reality of the world she finds herself in. Instead, the frigid December air is matched only by the "cold as stone" attitude the world has toward this throwaway kid. Grace is "lost and alone." Perhaps she finds herself exposed to an underworld of drugs, violence, and prostitution. Grace is hopeless and has nowhere to turn for help.

However, as desperate as the young runaway is, she doesn't even consider seeking help from Christians. "She'd never darken the door of any church," sings Point of Grace in the second verse. In his book *What's So Amazing about Grace?* Philip Yancey tells a similar true story about a down-and-out prostitute in downtown Chicago. She was asked if she had ever thought of going to a church for help. She responded, **"Church! Why would I ever go there? I was already feeling terrible about myself. They'd just make me feel worse."**[1]

What a far cry from the reaction that Jesus received during his ministry on earth! The prostitutes and Graces of the world flocked to Jesus; they never ran away from him. How could Christians—who are supposed to be the "body of Christ" to a hurting world—cause a completely opposite reaction?

Sadly, to Grace, the body of Christ looks much more like the judgmental church represented in the film *Chocolat*—one that will snap its teeth at you the moment you don't meet its strict moral standards. *Chocolat* is a story of a single mother named Vianne and her daughter, who wander from village to village in France in the 1950s. As the film begins, they move into a traditional French town that is controlled by the mayor. The mayor is not only the town administrator but also has an iron grip on the town's lone church. The mayor is initially friendly toward

Vianne; that is, until he discovers that she is an unwed mother and has no interest in attending church. After that, his goal is to get rid of this pollutant by running her out of town. The movie shows the stark contrast between the judgmentalism of the mayor and the grace shown by Vianne to everyone she meets, including eventually the mayor himself.

Stepping Out

The world hasn't always been like this. In a time not too long ago, the church was known far and wide as the place to turn to when you needed help. The classic story *Les Misérables* offers one of most powerful images in all of literature of the body of Christ in action.

Les Misérables tells the story of an ex-convict named Jean Valjean. Valjean was imprisoned in a labor camp for seventeen years for the trivial offense of stealing a single loaf of bread to feed his hungry family. As the story begins, Valjean has just been released from prison and is traveling through a small French town on a cold, rainy night. Earlier in the evening, Valjean sought shelter at the only inn around. But because his papers identified him as an ex-convict, he was turned away by the innkeeper. With nowhere else to turn, Valjean lays down on a lonely park bench in the town square.

Eventually a passerby awakens the drowsy Valjean and points him to the home of the local bishop to get out of the weather. In soggy desperation, Valjean knocks on the door and asks for a night's lodging, fully expecting to have the door slammed on him. Yet, amazingly, the bishop not only warmly invites him inside but serves him a hot meal using his finest silver and offers him a comfortable bed to sleep on.

Valjean, however, is much too hardened by his years in prison to feel any gratitude. He awakens in the middle of the night and

Living in the World

decides to steal the silverware. But his attempt proves clumsy: in his flight from town, he is caught by the police. Valjean claims innocence; the silverware was a gift from the bishop, he says. But the police don't buy the phony story and bring him back to the bishop's house in the morning, expecting to hear a much different version from the bishop himself.

When the bishop sees a handcuffed Valjean and the accompanying police and hears their charges, he does a most unexpected thing. Instead of crying, "Thief!" he looks at Valjean and asks him why he didn't take the silver candlesticks along with the silverware. Valjean is dumbfounded. He was expecting that the testimony of the bishop would send him back to his prison cell for good. Instead, the police remove the cuffs and say he is free to go.

Before Valjean can react, the bishop goes back into the house and brings out two silver candlesticks, the only property the bishop owned of any value at all. Placing them into the convict's hands, the bishop looks into the eyes of Valjean and says, "Jean Valjean, my brother: you belong no longer to evil, but to good. It is your soul I am buying for you."[2]

Les Misérables offers an incredible portrait of a Christian showing God's grace to those who most need it. However, what is so striking to me is that the story is outdated. It's unrealistic in today's world: a twenty-first-century Jean Valjean would never have even knocked at a bishop's door.

If we are like most Christians, we are so insulated from the Graces and Valjeans that they never come across our path or knock on our door. Part of this is geographical— most churches are in suburbia, comfortably away from the down-and-outs

A twenty-first-century Jean Valjean would never have even knocked at a bishop's door.

of society. Another part is the reputation that the church has today for being as judgmental as the mayor in *Chocolat*.

As a result, while the bishop might have been able to react and show Christ's love to people knocking, we have to go one step further: we have to be proactive and go looking for them. As the second verse of "Saving Grace" continues, Point of Grace sings about this reality:

> She'd never darken the door of any church
> She would say "What for?
> No one there would care for me"
> We have to go where she lives
> Simply show her who Jesus is
> Watch Him set her free
> For grace flows down from above
> And faith requires a selfless love
> For a world that's dying to see
> The hope in you in me

We have to go out into the world and look for Grace, because she is not going to come to us. As intimidating as this idea can be, our job is not hard once we take the first step. As Point of Grace sings, we "simply show her who Jesus is" by meeting her needs and loving her. We don't need to go through a six-week training program, be a Bible school graduate, or own a library of C. S. Lewis books. We simply need to care for her. That's showing her who Jesus is by our Christlike actions.

When serving Christ in this way, we can have a tremendous freedom. We don't need to worry about how successful we are: Grace's response is in God's hands. As Point of Grace sings, we can sit back and "watch Him set her free." Jesus Christ, not us, will do the work inside of Grace. As we are obedient to Christ, his "grace flows down from above." He will work through our "selfless love" as we minister to people who are "dying to see the hope" that only Jesus Christ offers.

Living Out Christ's Call

Comfy is the last word that would have ever been used to describe the church of the New Testament. The early church was famous the world over for sacrificial love and generosity even in the midst of persecution by others around them. They were able to spread the gospel at record speed because their faith was active, sacrificial, and outward focused.

The chorus of "Saving Grace" describes how to live out these principles of the New Testament church today. Point of Grace sings:

> It's all about saving Grace
> All about living love
> Being Jesus
> To those he came to save
> Sharing life
> And giving our own away
> All about serving God
> All about saving Grace

In these lyrics, Point of Grace lays out a road map for how we can reach out to a lost world.

First, we must share God's "saving grace" with others around us. Point of Grace sings, "It's all about saving Grace." Here *Grace* has two meanings: the runaway girl described in the song and God's "saving grace," which is the heart of the gospel. All we do should be centered on this saving grace of Jesus Christ; we shouldn't get sidetracked on unimportant issues that don't matter in the long run.

Second, we must focus on the needs of the Graces of the world. The line "It's all about saving Grace" also reminds us that our responsibility as disciples is "saving Grace," the runaway girl, and those like her. But our mission is more than just evangelizing her; it is loving her exactly where she is at. In *Les Misérables*, for example, when the bishop has dinner with Valjean on their night together, he is low-key about things. He doesn't try to preach "the four spiritual laws" and have Valjean converted before dessert. Instead, the bishop simply gives him a good meal and recognizes that Valjean's greatest need is something extremely common: to forget, even if for just an hour or so, his hard and difficult life. The bishop thought that Valjean had his misery on his mind constantly. Therefore, rather than ask him about his life, it was best to avoid any mention of his past. Perhaps it would help him feel just like everyone, even if only for a moment, to be treated in this ordinary way. The bishop believes that this is really at the heart of what Christ's love is all about. He concludes: "Is there not something truly evangelical in avoiding the sermonizing and moralizing . . . and simply not touching on his suffering at all?"[3] The bishop understood that since his calling was "all about saving Valjean," his focus needed to be purely on Valjean's needs, not on a preplanned agenda.

Third, we must demonstrate love in our daily lives. When we sincerely love others around us, we are living out a fundamental part of the gospel. During Christ's ministry, he often spoke against the Pharisees and the teachers of the law. He was not blasting them as perverts or closet adulterers. Instead, Christ was condemning the Pharisees because they didn't care about, to use Point of Grace's words, "living love." They were far more concerned about living comfortably away from the riffraff of society and appearing to be holy. Yet Jesus, saving his harshest words for them, called the Pharisees "whitewashed tombs" (Matt. 23:27). Without love, Jesus was saying, your faith is dead. To prevent this same Pharisee mentality from becoming part of us, we have to prioritize putting others' needs in front of our own, starting in our home and then reaching out to neighbors and strangers around us.

Fourth, we must be Jesus to others around us. Point of Grace sings that our role is "being Jesus to those He came to save." In other words, we are to assume the role of Jesus as we live our lives. The challenge of Point of Grace goes one step further than the familiar "WWJD?" lingo. We are not just doing what Jesus would do but actually *becoming* Jesus as we help others.

If we are "being Jesus," then we are going to be concerned about the same people Christ was concerned about during his earthly ministry. He didn't spend much time hanging out with the comfy Pharisees and church leaders. Instead, he got his hands dirty healing the sick, feeding the hungry, and simply loving the ones least respected in society.

Fifth, we are to give our lives away. As the chorus continues, Point of Grace sings that we are called to "sharing life and giving our own away." Rather than being concerned with our needs in our comfortable Christian mini-world, we need to share the hope we have in Christ and sacrifice our concerns for the concerns of others.

Point of Grace sings of the hurting girl, "God is counting on us to reach her with His love." God is calling us, as members of the body of Christ, to live out these five principles sung about in the chorus. We are called to be his arms and legs to the "count-less millions just like Grace who need a merciful embrace." As

Point of Grace reminds us, "They won't believe our God is real until they feel His touch."

Being Jesus

Consider the story of a young, cowardly soldier named Alexander who served under Alexander the Great, one of the greatest military leaders in history. The soldier was brought before the mighty general to face punishment for his gutless actions. Towering over the coward, Alexander the Great asked him, "What is your name, soldier?" The solder replied, "Alexander, Your Highness." Enraged by this answer, the general asked the man two more times to state his name. But each time, the same reply was given. After the soldier responded a third time, Alexander the Great looked him straight in the eye and said with a burning fury, "Soldier, either change your behavior or change your name."

In much the same way, when we call ourselves Christians, we are taking on Christ's name. Or, in the words of Point of Grace, we are actually "being Jesus to those He came to save." But, as the Alexander the Great story challenges, are we living up to that name? Are we reaching out for Grace? And when she sees us, does she run to us like she would to Christ? Or is she repelled by just another churchgoer?

C. S. Lewis once said that for every person you encounter in your day, you either lead them one step closer to heaven or one step closer to hell. The Graces of the world are all around you. You will encounter them. The only question is on which of these two paths you will lead them.

SAVING GRACE
by Point of Grace

She had her father's blue eyes
He left home before she arrived
Mama named her Grace
Just getting by on their own
When Grace was fifteen she ran from home
One December day Grace is lost and alone
In a world as cold as stone
God is counting on us
To reach her with His love

[Chorus:]
It's all about saving grace
All about living love
Being Jesus to those he came to save
Sharing life
And giving our own away
It's all about serving God
All about saving Grace

She'd never darken the door of any church
She would say, "what for?
No one there would care for me"
We have to go where she lives
Simply show her who Jesus is
Watch Him set her free
For grace flows down from above
And faith requires a selfless love
For a world that's dying to see
The hope in you in me

[Chorus]

There are countless millions just like Grace
Who need a merciful embrace
They won't believe our God is real
Until they feel his touch

★ ★ ★ diving deeper ★ ★ ★

Read *What's So Amazing About Grace?* by Philip Yancey, a highly readable book that will forever change your understanding of what grace is.

Read *Les Misérables* by Victor Hugo, or watch a film version such as the 1998 release starring Liam Neeson.

Read Bruce Marchiano's *In the Footsteps of Jesus* to gain insight into the heart and mind of Jesus Christ and his genuine love for others. Bruce played Jesus in the Visual Bible's *The Gospel of Matthew* and shares the spiritual journey he encountered during the filming of this video.

Action Steps

In "Saving Grace," Point of Grace challenges you to reach out to people who most need God's grace. As you think about your response, consider the following action steps:

Offer your life to God and ask him to use you to reach out to the Graces and Jean Valjeans of the world. Specifically pray that God would open up opportunities for you to minister to others.

Identify needs in your area, whether they are in your town or a nearby inner city. Consider how you can get involved with an existing organization or whether God is calling you to venture out on your own to meet needs that are being overlooked.

No matter your age, don't take a backseat. Spearhead the charge in your local church to reach out, both locally and to other parts of the world.

Read through the Gospel of Matthew focusing on the way that Jesus interacted and treated people. Then get practical and live out that same love in your life.

Watch Les Misérables (I recommend the 1998 film version) and see God's transforming power in the life of Jean Valjean.

18

A Modern Pharisee

People who know God's truth can have a nasty side to them. Don't get me wrong—when we really grasp what Jesus Christ did for us on the cross, we will have a deep sense of humility and gratitude. But if we lose touch with that reality, then we can begin to believe that we somehow earned our standing as a "child of God." When this happens, our Christian faith becomes a perch from which to look down upon and categorize the "lost of the world." Muslims become fanatics. Buddhists have their heads in the clouds, while atheists have theirs in the sand. Jews, well, they are just trying to relive the glory days of the Old Testament. Without even realizing it, we begin to look upon people who are different from us with a sense of smugness and an air of superiority.

we begin to look upon people who are different from us with a sense of smugness and an air of superiority.

In her song "Wide Eyed," Nichole Nordeman sings about how this arrogance can creep into our Christian walk. Nordeman compares this attitude with the chief opposition Jesus faced during his earthly ministry—the Pharisees. She sings that when we start to believe we're better than others, we become, in effect, modern-day Pharisees. Not only do we behave the opposite of how Jesus behaved, but we actually become a tool of Satan working against the very God we claim to be serving.

Nordeman wrote "Wide Eyed" as a result of her experience of living in Hollywood. Nordeman says that before that time she lived a sheltered, safe Christian life, surrounded by people much like herself. But during her stay in "Tinseltown," she was convicted by the fact that she found herself quick to judge others and look down on those who, in her own words, "threatened my sense of normalcy."[1]

Different Strokes

In the first two verses of "Wide Eyed," Nordeman sings about two very different people she encounters—people quite unlike any others she had come across in her sanitized past. Nordeman first sees a man on a downtown street who "was preaching to a mailbox down on 16th Avenue." The man claimed "he was Jesus, sent from Jupiter to free us." And "with a bottle of tequila and one shoe," the man "raged about repentance." Then, as she sings in the second verse, Nordeman interacts with a woman in a bookstore who was into New Age-y stuff. She was thumbing through a yoga magazine and started talking to Nordeman about her past life as a "plantation slave's wife" and the crystals that gave her life balance and meaning.

You have probably been in situations like Nordeman was in, where you encountered a person who was not who you expected. Maybe it was a man in the park wearing a "Repent! The end is near!" placard and screaming at you as you walked by. A neighbor down the street who has always been something of an oddball. Or a kid at school who is a social outcast. When we encounter a person who goes against our sense of what is normal, we can find it natural to act just like Nordeman did: being "wide eyed in disbelief and disillusion" and "tongue tied, drawn by my conclusions." In other words, some people don't fit into our understanding of how the world should be or how people should act. So when they invade our comfort zone, we can have a hard time dealing with it.

When we encounter people who are "different," a natural response is to look down on them. This smugness expresses itself in a variety of ways. First, we can ignore or blow off someone who is unlike us. That's what Nordeman did to the man on the sidewalk; she "turned and walked away" and "casually dismissed him as a fraud." She responded the same way to the woman in the bookstore, leaving her with a patronizing "Sounds nice" reply. **We can also take that arrogant attitude a step further and actually laugh at and mock the person we deem unusual.** Nordeman confesses that she found herself doing that, as she laughed at what both people had to say. Finally, we can look down on and avoid people when we are scared of them. People with disabilities or those who just look different experience this reaction from others all the time. Suppose, for example, you see a visitor in church who is severely scarred or disfigured. Do you rush to welcome her? Or do you try to avoid eye contact and dart quickly around the corner? If we avoid her, we may not be mocking her, but we are still treating her differently because she doesn't fit into our sense of what is normal.

In contrast, during his earthly ministry, Jesus's idea of what is common or ordinary was far broader than what we may be used to. Jesus never wrote anyone off. Instead, he loved being around all sorts of people and valued them simply for who they were. When Jesus healed a man with leprosy, he didn't do it with a ten-foot pole; he reached out and touched the man. When Jesus socialized, he had dinner with the lowlifes and outcasts, not the rich and famous of Israel. When Jesus came across a demon-possessed wild man, he didn't run and hide; he had compassion and healed the man.

A Different Sort of Savior

In the third verse of "Wide Eyed," Nordeman compares how she behaved toward the man and the New Ager with the way the Pharisees treated Jesus. The lyrics start out like this:

Not so long ago, a man from Galilee
Fed thousands with His bread and His theology
And the truth He spoke
Quickly became the joke
Of educated, self-inflated Pharisees like me

The Pharisees were the religious leaders of the day, the elite of Jewish society. They saw themselves as the models for how everyone should live and became fanatical about keeping to their long lists of do's and don'ts. The Pharisees claimed to dedicate their lives to serving God but somehow had gotten terribly distracted in the process. They cared more and more about "looking good" in front of others and less and less about what really matters to God. Perhaps their unspoken motto was "It's better to look good than be good."

And so when this simple carpenter named Jesus came along and claimed he was the Messiah, the Pharisees didn't know what to do. Instead of focusing on outward behavior, Jesus kept talking about the condition of one's heart before God. Jesus didn't fit into the Pharisees' concept of normalcy. So they dismissed him. Mocked him. Laughed at him. In their closed-mindedness, the Pharisees would not even consider the possibility that Jesus might be telling them the truth, that he could be who he claimed to be.

When dealing with Jesus, the Pharisees were "wide eyed in disbelief and disillusion / They were tongue tied, drawn by their conclusions." In spite of the fact that Jesus backed up his teaching of Scripture with miracles, their hearts were hardened to anything that didn't conform to their definition of who the Messiah was supposed to be. They envisioned an elite, powerful leader, undoubtedly rising from among the Pharisees themselves.

As Nichole Nordeman shows in "Wide Eyed," she was struck by the parallels between how she behaved toward certain people she encountered in Hollywood and the Pharisees' treatment of Jesus Christ. Wondering how she would have reacted to Jesus Christ if she had met him on a downtown street, she asks herself:

Would I have turned and walked away
And laughed at what He had to say
And casually dismissed Him as a fraud
Unaware that I was staring at the image of
my God

While Nordeman speculates on what she would have done if she came across Jesus today, the real heartbreaker of the last verse of "Wide Eyed" is that the Pharisees actually responded to Jesus in this way. They mocked and scorned Jesus and sent him to his death although he was innocent. And as they looked at Jesus hanging on the cross, they were "unaware that [they were] staring at the image of [their] God." Because of their hard hearts, they became Satan's tool in killing off the God they said they were serving.

When we read the Gospel accounts of Jesus's life and the behavior of the Pharisees, it's easy to look down on the religious leaders and dismiss them as fools for crucifying the Son of God. Yet Nordeman's point in this verse is that when we have an air of superiority in our attitude toward different people, we take on that same Pharisee-like attitude.

Sheep and Goats

In Matthew 25, Jesus tells his followers the story of the sheep and the goats. Jesus says that when he returns again, he will put people into two groups: the sheep on his right and the goats on

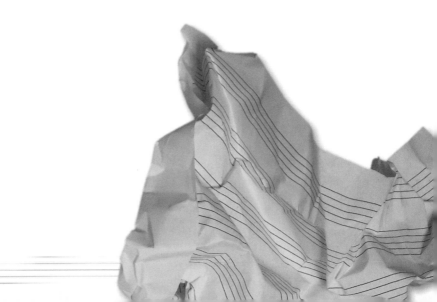

his left. Jesus will welcome the sheep into his future kingdom because they were the ones who did such things as give him something to eat when he was hungry, invite him in when he was a stranger, and care for him when he was sick. In contrast, Jesus tells the goats essentially to get lost because they didn't feed him, invite him in, or care for him. Both groups were clueless, because they didn't recall doing any of this to Jesus, until he said, "Whatever you did for one of the least of these brothers of mine, you did for me" (v. 40).

When we dismiss, mock, or are scared to be around a person who is different from us, then we, like Nordeman, forget that he was created in the image of our God. In other words, yes, how we act toward the mentally disturbed man, the New Ager, the oddball neighbor, and the social outcast is how we are acting toward Jesus Christ himself.

WIDE EYED
by Nichole Nordeman

When I met him on a sidewalk
He was preaching to a mailbox
Down on 16th Avenue
And he told me he was Jesus
Sent from Jupiter to free us
With a bottle of tequila and one shoe
He raged about repentance
He finished every sentence
With a promise that the end was close at hand
I didn't even try to understand

He left me wide eyed in disbelief and disillusion
I was tongue tied, drawn by my conclusions
So I turned and walked away
And laughed at what he had to say
Then casually dismissed him as a fraud
I forgot he was created in the image of my God

When I met her in a bookstore
She was browsing on the first floor
Through a yoga magazine
And she told me in her past life
She was some plantation slave's wife
She had to figure out what that might mean
She believes the healing powers of her crystals
Can bring balance and new purpose to her life
Sounds nice

She left me wide eyed in disbelief and
disillusion
I was tongue tied, drawn by my conclusions
So I turned and walked away
And laughed at what she had to say
Then casually dismissed her as a fraud
I forgot she was created in the image of my
God

Not so long ago, a man from Galilee
Fed thousands with His bread and His theology
And the truth He spoke
Quickly became the joke
Of educated, self-inflated Pharisees like me

And they were wide eyed in disbelief and
disillusion
They were tongue tied, drawn by their
conclusions
Would I have turned and walked away
And laughed at what He had to say
And casually dismissed Him as a fraud
Unaware that I was staring at the image of my
God

Used by permission. [27]

★ ★ ★ **diving deeper** ★ ★ ★

Read Matthew 8:1–4; 9:1–2; 9:9–13; 17:14–18; and 25:31–46.

A Modern Pharisee

Action Steps

In "Wide Eyed," Nichole Nordeman sings about the smug attitude Christians can have when people are different from what we expect. As you explore the lyrics to this song, consider the following steps:

- Examine your heart when you are around someone who is "different." Do you mock, ignore, or avoid them? Or do you love them like you would a longtime friend? Ask for help from God to treat them as Jesus would.

- If you live a sheltered, safe Christian life like Nichole did, prayerfully consider taking on ministry opportunities that put you in firsthand encounters with people who are not like you.

19

A Noisy Walk

Step inside a movie theater after a tiring, hectic day, and you'll see the truth of the expression "Art imitates life." A cutting-edge filmmaking technique seen in such films as *The Bourne Supremacy* is bringing the frantic pace of real life to the big screen. In place of stationary cameras and long shots, some filmmakers are now using hand-held cameras, half-focused shots, split-second edits, and constant camera movements. The result is a jittery, chaotic experience that will leave you either exhilarated in your seat or nauseous on the floor. This realistic style of filmmaking, popularly known as *cinema verité*, is a far cry from the ordinary "point and shoot" techniques of days gone by. What's more significant, however, is that this style also reveals something about the society in which we live today. **The slow-paced life of the past has been transformed into a world resembling a high-tech, nonstop action film.**

In their song "Adding to the Noise," Switchfoot sings about the problems that this frenzied lifestyle can wreak in your Christian walk. The band offers a biting commentary on modern culture, all the while reminding that their music should not become yet another distraction.

Breathless

As Switchfoot begins "Adding to the Noise," they issue a wake-up call. They challenge us to think about what we are doing to slow the relentless pace of a lifestyle that leaves us out of breath:

What's it gonna take
To slow us down

To let the silence spin us around?
What's it gonna take
To drop this town?
We've been spinning at the speed of sound

Perhaps modern society has taken the label associated with New York—"the city that never sleeps"—and run with it. Nothing comes to a standstill anymore. No one ever sleeps. The world is "spinning at the speed of sound" and seems impossible to stop. Once in a while a tragedy like 9/11 or the Southeast Asian tsunami sobers everyone up . . . for a time. Yet that brief pause doesn't seem to last very long. People soon get on with their lives, winding the world up tight for yet another spin.

But the rapid pace of the world is only part of the issue. After all, if you are all by yourself on a highway, you can drive at almost any speed, fast or slow, without too much bother. But once you have other cars and semitrucks around you, your pace makes all the difference. If you go too fast, you will collide with others. Go too slow and you'll get rear-ended. Better to go the same speed and hope for the best. In the same way, contemporary life offers more challenges than just its sheer speed. There are constant potholes we have to dodge along the way. Switchfoot sings of these distractions:

Stepping out of those convenience stores
What could we want but more, more, more?
From the third world
To the corporate core
We are the symphony of modern humanity

When we go into a convenience store or a shopping mall, our selfish, sinful nature will leave us dissatisfied with what we own and make us want "more, more, more." The impulse buy. The deal of the century. The sale you couldn't afford to turn down. Instead of carefully considering and praying about what we purchase, our bottom line is often whether or not our checking account or credit line can handle it. And even when we are trying to avoid materialism, the difference between what we "need" and what we "want" is often quite hazy.

While those of us in America may be more exposed to this temptation than someone living in the third world, the planet is growing small enough that most everyone feels the effects of commercialism. In fact, the worldwide nature of the Internet makes our location less important than ever before. Don't live near a mall? No problem. You can access Amazon.com or bargain hunt on the Web just as easily in Lusk, Wyoming, as you can in downtown Manhattan. The "symphony of modern humanity" keeps harmony to this endless chorus of "more, more, more."

These things we buy promise to make life better, but they usually don't. In reality, they simply add another layer of distraction to our frazzled lives. "I don't know what they're gonna think of next," sings Switchfoot of those "genetic engineers of the most high tech." More technologies, whether in medicine or entertainment, are developed to soothe or amuse us, to keep us from doing anything but actually face head-on the pressures of modern life. But since these inventions aren't free, Switchfoot points out that people are more than willing to offer us "a couple new ways to fall into debt" to pay

our selfish, sinful nature will leave us dissatisfied with what we own and make us want "more, more."

for them. Then, when our stress and money problems start to spiral out of control, modern life offers one more escape: "that TV set tells us what we've wanted to hear," leaving us numb and pacified, says Switchfoot.

iNoise

The frantic pace and constant distractions of the twenty-first century can make our Christian walk a noisy one, one in which we find it difficult to hear God. In fact, in this day and age, I bet that you can go through an entire day without hearing any silence whatsoever. You can be awakened to the buzz of an alarm clock, watch the news and traffic report at breakfast, and listen to talk radio on your commute to school or work. While there, you multitask—talking on your cell phone about a new project while you Internet chat with a buddy. In the afternoon, you are stressed out, so you manage to get away from everyone for a jog in the park. But instead of peace and quiet, you listen nonstop to blaring Switchfoot tunes on your iPod. Feeling hungry, you go out to eat with some friends, then quickly skip home to watch a couple of sitcoms. Finally, feeling exhausted from the day's hectic pace, you fall asleep listening to your favorite punk CD.

In contemporary society, **noise is emerging as one of Satan's most effective weapons** to sidetrack us from our relationship with Christ. C. S. Lewis illustrates this in *The Screwtape Letters*, a fictional account of a senior demon writing to a junior demon about how to tempt human beings. In one letter Screwtape, the senior devil, expresses his hatred of music and silence; he sees this combination as deadly effective in leading people toward God. In their place, Screwtape says, must come noise. He writes:

Music and silence—how I detest them both! How thankful we should be that ever since [Satan] entered Hell . . . no square inch of infernal space and no moment of infernal time has been surrendered to either of those abominable forces, but all has been occupied by Noise—Noise, the grand dynamism, the audible expression of all that is exultant, ruthless, and virile . . . We will make the whole universe a noise in the end.[1]

In a world that always needs something on, noise is such an effective weapon because it drowns out God's voice. But when we look in the Bible, we discover that God speaks in the midst of silence, not through constant clatter. Verse after verse, we read of the need to be silent before the Lord. "Be still, and know that I am God," says Psalm 46:10. Zechariah 2:13 adds, "Be still before the LORD, all mankind." The Old Testament prophet Elijah certainly discovered this truth. All alone in the wilderness and desperately needing to hear from God, he saw God's power in a windstorm, an earthquake, and a fire. Yet God didn't speak to Elijah through these mighty acts of nature. Instead, 1 Kings 19:12 says that God spoke to the prophet through "a gentle whisper" that followed. God much prefers a murmur to a megaphone.

Jesus understood the importance of silence during his time on earth. He may not have had a cell phone or pager to contend with, but he did have to deal with distractions even more demanding—and ones that he couldn't just turn off or set to "vibrate" mode. A never-ending flood of people followed Jesus wherever he traveled. They all wanted something from him: teaching, preaching, healing, or feeding. During Christ's three-year ministry on earth, noise was a 24/7 issue for him.

Never one to get stressed out, Jesus responded to the noise by periodically sneaking off on his own to be alone and silent in prayer. Jesus was realistic: he knew that doing God's will meant

Living in the World

he couldn't just run away from the noise. But he made sure that he'd control the distractions rather than letting them control him. Jesus understood that silent moments wouldn't be there unless he was proactive and created them himself. Similarly, if we are going to follow Christ's command to be in the world but not of the world (John 17:15–17), we are going to have to deal with the issue of noise. But, like Christ, we will have to create silent moments ourselves, not expect them to naturally appear in the pages of our planners.

Christianized Noise

Because of the havoc that noise can cause in our walk with Christ, the chorus of "Adding to the Noise" warns us to make sure that music, like anything else, doesn't distract us from what's most important:

If we're adding to the noise
Turn off this song
If we're adding to the noise
Turn off your stereo, radio, video

In other words, Switchfoot is saying that if they are a stumbling block to hearing God, we should turn them off. The band recognizes that even things labeled "Christian" can sometimes only serve to add another layer of noise to our busy lives. In fact, we can easily fill our lives with all things Christian—listening to Christian music, reading Christian books, and participating in endless Christian activities—all the while ignoring our spiritual life with Christ. These Christian things are good when they supplement a balanced life. But if we overdose on them, they just become "Christianized noise."

We can seek peace in "more," but we will only find less. We can chat all day and night, but we will only gain loneliness. We can escape into a high-tech heaven, but we'll only win the emptiness of hell. In the opening lines of the song, Switchfoot asks, "What's it gonna take" to slow down our lives in the midst of this noise. If we look honestly at our lives and consider that question, we may find ourselves feeling as nauseous as watching a *cinema verité* film. But if we commit to regularly seeking God's silence, then we'll find ourselves, like Jesus, amazingly able to cope with the complexities and distractions of modern life.

God will never scream at you with a megaphone over the racket. He'll speak to you softly, all the while hoping you'll stop and hear. Now's the time . . .

Mute your iPod.

Turn off your cell.

And simply be still before your Savior.

He's waiting.

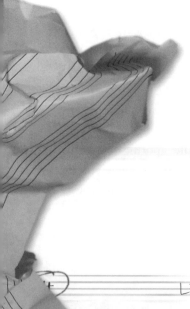

ADDING TO THE NOISE
by Switchfoot

What's it gonna take
To slow us down
To let the silence spin us around?
What's it gonna take
To drop this town?
We've been spinning at the speed of sound

Stepping out of those convenience stores
What could we want but more, more, more?
From the third world
To the corporate core
We are the symphony of modern humanity

If we're adding to the noise
Turn off this song
If we're adding to the noise
Turn off your stereo, radio, video

I don't know
what they're gonna think of next
Genetic engineers of the most high tech
A couple new ways
To fall into debt
I'm a nervous wreck but I'll bet
That that TV set
Tells us what we've wanted to hear
But none of these sound bites
Are coming in clear
From the third world to the corporate ear
We are the symphony of modern humanity

Used by permission. [23]

★ ★ ★ diving deeper ★ ★ ★
Read Exodus 14:14; 1 Kings 19:11–13; Psalms 37:7; 46:10;
Zechariah 2:12–13; Matthew 14:23–24; Luke 4:42.

Action Steps

In "Adding to the Noise," Switchfoot challenges you to think about the distractions and pace of your life. As you reflect on the song, prayerfully consider the following steps:

- Set aside a low-tech day and get away from your cell phone, radio, iPod, TV, and other high-tech gadgets. Then, in the silence, listen for God's voice. Next, go one step further: Get away from TV, movies, and other distractions for a week. Spend extra time in the Bible and in prayer during the week; you'll be amazed how much you can grow in your Christian walk in just seven days.

- Carve out a specific time every day for personal time with God. Start out with just 15 minutes in the morning or evening and then expand to 30 minutes or more as you feel ready.

- Don't expect silence to come your way. Like Christ, you have to create your silent moments. Start out with small but concrete steps, such as avoiding the radio if you normally wake up to music or turning off the television during dinner.

2
The
Simple
Life

The Next Big Thing comes in all shapes and sizes. Whether it is a high-tech digital gadget, a thinner television, or a hipper car, there's always a hot product that people just have to buy. Demand soars and supplies become scarce, and customers scour the city trying to find a store that hasn't sold out of their last shipment. Our economy is powered by the Next Big Thing.

Contentment is always just around the corner.

But the problem with the Next Big Thing is that contentment is always just around the corner. We see an emptiness in our lives and convince ourselves that we can only fill it by buying whatever is the latest craze. This desire first surfaces when we are young. Toys, dolls, and video games are the usual starter pack. Then as we get older, clothes, cell phones, and MP3 players begin to take center stage. By the time we settle down with a family at thirty-something, we're ready for the big leagues: luxury SUVs and big houses in the suburbs.

In a world drowning in this sea of materialism, Audio Adrenaline's song "Chevette" offers a breath of fresh air. On the surface, "Chevette" is an airy, fun tune about a family car that lead singer Mark Stuart had growing up. But underneath the song's apparent fluff is a deeper message for disciples living in this material world: there is an alternative to the lifestyle of the Next Big Thing, a simple life with freedom and no regrets.

Living Simply

As "Chevette" begins, Audio Adrenaline takes us back to one of those special family memories that you probably had as a kid growing up—the first time you saw the new family car. The first verse starts off like this:

> Twenty years ago I watched in awe
> As my dad drove up the driveway
> More than proud to have a brand new family car

Listening to the song for the first time and hearing that Mark "watched in awe" as his dad drove the car up, one might assume the vehicle is a luxury car. A Porsche, Corvette, or Beamer perhaps. But as the song continues, we start to catch on to his joke: it's no fancy European import at all but a subcompact, economy car—and one of questionable reliability at that. It gets "thirty miles to the gallon" and can go from zero to sixty "sometimes." Yet those shortcomings did not dampen the enthusiasm of Mark and his family. They looked past all that and were simply "in awe" of actually owning a "brand new family car."

Instead of being unhappy with the things the car lacked (which was most everything), Mark took the one true feature that the vehicle did have—a hatchback—and made the most of it. Mark sings that as his dad drove down the highway,

> I remember putting down the back seat
> And lying in the hatchback
> Looking at the sky watching trees go by

Mark is speaking of experiences in his past that are quite divorced from the world of the Next Big Thing. It's a glimpse of the simple life, a way of life in which we deliberately live with less so we can give more of ourselves to Jesus Christ.

As the song continues, we discover that Mark was a PK, a preacher's kid. If you are a PK or have a friend who is one, you immediately understand what that means: financial sacrifice as the whole family serves God. But while there may not have been much extra cash lying around the house, that didn't seem to matter to Mark. Instead, he saw his dad as a rich man where it most counted:

> I was the son of a preacher
> And he was a rich poor man

As a pastor, Mark's father was not wealthy from the world's perspective, but he was well-off in God's eyes. Jesus says in Luke 6:20, "Blessed are you who are poor, for yours is the kingdom of God." Reading this verse, we might be tempted to set aside these blessings as only for the future, saved for heaven. But Mark's family offers proof that these blessings also can be experienced in the here and now. By living simple lives dedicated to God, we may have lightweight pocketbooks, but we will be weighed down with spiritual blessings that the latest hot product can never give: contentment, peace, joy, and freedom.

In spite of the joy a simple life brings, the journey for the disciple is not an easy, tame ride. Audio Adrenaline brings us back down to earth in the second verse:

> The winter cracked the highway
> And we tried to dodge the potholes
> He never promised us it would be a gentle ride

Mark's family car, a 1977 Chevy Chevette, did not have a reputation for offering its passengers the ultimate ride experience. In fact, if you drove on a highway of potholes, you might find your body experiencing aftershocks long after you stepped out of the car. That the Chevette never gave Mark and his family a "gentle ride" parallels the bumpy road that was their simple life. A life of simplicity is difficult because it requires a constant commitment to live out Christ's call to die to ourselves. When friends rave about the Next Big Thing, for example, we may have to sit on the sidelines and remind ourselves of what is really important. It's easy to be strong for a while, but that strength can wear down over time. If we start to take our eyes off of Jesus Christ, our attitude spirals downward. We become resentful and feel like we are being cheated. Our simple life quickly degenerates into a sulky life.

Yet in spite of the potholes and temptations, Mark's father stood firm. He kept his focus consistently on Jesus Christ:

He never had a problem though
Keeping it on the narrow road

Jesus talks about this "narrow road" in Matthew 7:13–14. He tells his followers to avoid the crowded wide lanes that lead to destruction and ruin. Instead, walk down the narrow road, says Jesus. It's the one path that leads to life, though only a handful of people find it.

No Regrets

A television commercial ran a few years ago that depicted a man looking back with amusement on the '70s fashions and fads that he used to think were big stuff. Indeed, when we look back at what was once important to us, the memories can be quite humorous. A once-fashionable dress is now an eyesore hanging in the back of your closet. The exercise machine that was intended to get you in great shape sits atrophying in the basement. The top-of-the-line VCR you paid top dollar for gathers dust next to your shiny new DVD player. We can look back at these kinds of purchases and shake our heads in embarrassment with a forced smile over how silly we were. But this stuff can also leave us with a bad taste in our mouths: regrets over the money wasted and the sacrifices made in order to pay for those now worthless items. The wide road of the Next Big Thing leaves a trail of regret as we look back on it.

Consider, however, the alternative reality—what it feels like to look at the "narrow road" in your rearview mirror. Mark's reminisces about his family car from twenty years ago provide a unique way to look at the simple life through the eyes of someone who actually lived it. As Mark relives these childhood memories, he finds enjoyment in describing just how plain a car the Chevette was. He starts off in the first chorus with:

No A.C.
And no FM

And then in the last chorus, he adds to it:

I had no A.C.
In my Chevette
Had window cranks
In my Chevette
Had vinyl seats
In my Chevette

The Chevette had just an AM radio. It had window cranks instead of power windows and vinyl seats in place of leather ones. And yet, in spite of the car's inadequacies, Mark's next line tells the real story:

And no regrets
In my Chevelle

As is made clear in the song, Mark never would have exchanged the simple life of his family for the privilege and wealth of a millionaire's home. He takes pleasure in the fact that he grew up in this sacrificial lifestyle. Mark can look back at the old clunker of a car today with a smile on his face. He sings, "Poor thing is up on blocks / but that car still rocks." When we live a simple life, we can look back with a smile—not one of embarrassment but one of joy.

Most importantly, Mark sings that he has "no regrets." He never felt deprived. Never believed he was missing out on important things that other kids had growing up. He shows only a quiet sense of gratitude to his father for leading his family down the "narrow road."

Simply Put

As disciples living in this materialistic world, we can easily give lip service to the idea of a simpler life yet continue to live straddling the highway—with one foot on the narrow road and one foot on the wide lane. That awkward position is exactly where Satan wants us. He will give us one foot on Christ's road because he knows that in that position, we will justify to ourselves that we are doing the best we can in this complex world. What's more, Satan knows that the wide road seduces us more and more the longer we have one foot on each path. Therefore, in order to live in simplicity, we need to actively decide to put both feet on Christ's path and leave the other road in the rearview mirror. To do so, we must prayerfully make the following three commitments.

First, realize that we need less to live on than we think we do. When we see a new sweater at The Gap or a cutting edge PDA at Best Buy, we can feel our pulse racing. But when this happens, we need to ask ourselves whether we *need* it or just *want* it. Keep in mind a quote from the film *Sabrina*: "More isn't always better. Sometimes it's just more." As Mark discovered, we can make it just fine going through the world with less—without FM, power windows, or leather seats.

Second, we must focus our eyes on God's narrow road, not on the Next Big Thing. Satan uses materialism as one of the greatest snares of the modern age. In 1 Timothy 6, the apostle Paul warns the early church of the danger of money. To paraphrase verses 9 and 10 for this day and age, "People who want the Next Big Thing fall into temptation and into many foolish and harmful desires that ultimately plunge them into ruin and destruction. . . . Some people, eager for the Next Big Thing, have wandered from the faith and pierced themselves with many griefs."

Your mind is the field of a battle between God and Satan, who are vying for your soul. Given that, be careful what you let your mind daydream about. If you struggle with materialism, do as the apostle Paul recommends you do: flee temptation! Getting practical, that means that you should spend less time walking the mall or browsing Amazon.com. Instead, find your own way to stay well away from temptation, like "lying in the hatchback, looking at the sky, watching trees go by."

Third, we should remember that the more we have, the more we are enslaved by our possessions. The earthly baggage we own has to be carried along with us, not only physically but also financially. As a result, the simple truth is that when we have a lot of stuff, we have less freedom to serve God. Instead of being able to respond to God's call to go the mission field at a moment's notice, we can find ourselves trapped in our jobs just so we can pay our credit card bills and monthly car payments.

However, a simple life frees us from that bondage. Oswald Chambers was one disciple who saw the amazing freedom that the simple life provided him. He said, "It is a great thing to be detached enough from possessions so as not to be held by them, because when called to uproot it is done with little real trouble, and one realizes how gloriously possible it is."[1] Chambers understood exactly that the more we own, the more we become held by our possessions, so much so that they can dictate what we can and cannot do for God.

CHEVETTE
by Audio Adrenaline

Twenty years ago I watched in awe
As my dad drove up the driveway
More than proud to have a brand new family car
Thirty miles to the gallon
0 to 60, sometimes
I remember putting down the back seat
And lying in the hatchback
Looking at the sky, watching trees go by
I was the son of a preacher
And he was a rich poor man

No A.C.
And no FM
And no regrets
In my Chevette
Yeah
In my Chevette

The winter cracked the highway
And we tried to dodge the potholes
He never promised us it would be a gentle ride
He never had a problem though
Keeping it on the narrow road

No A.C.
And no FM
And no regrets
In my Chevette
Yeah
In my Chevette

Poor thing is up on blocks
But that car still
Rocks

Seems like yesterday
(Seems like yesterday, seems like yesterday)

My Chevette
Yeah
In my Chevette
Yeah
I had no A.C.
In my Chevette
Had window cranks
In my Chevette
Had vinyl seats
In my Chevette
In my Chevette
And no regrets
In my Chevette

Used by permission.

Action Steps

Audio Adrenaline's "Chevette" shows a way of life that is worlds apart from the "buy it now" society that we live in. Examine your heart today and determine whether you have fully given over your wallet to God. As you do so, consider the following action steps:

Commit yourself to a simple life so you can not only be free to serve God but also experience the blessings that God has for you.

Pray before purchases. Make it a practice that before you get out your wallet, you stop and wait. If you feel rushed, walk away because you know that impulse is from Satan, not God. Specifically pray about your purchase, and wait until you hear from God before you take action. Then when you do hear back from him, have the strength and determination to walk away if he says no.

Avoid temptation. Stay away from constant trips to the mall or browsing Amazon.com and other stores on the Web.

★ ★ ★ diving deeper ★ ★ ★

Read Matthew 7:13–14; Luke 6:20; 18:18–27; 1 Timothy 6:6–10; James 1:11; Revelation 2:9.

... in the World

Afterword

C. S. Lewis once wrote that reading books allowed him to become a thousand men and yet remain himself. The more we listen to Christian music, the more we can begin to understand what Lewis meant by that. For whenever we hear a great song like those we've looked at in *The Gospel Unplugged*, we discover that we can be forever changed. We begin to see the world, God, and even ourselves differently—through the eyes of the artist rather than just our own limited perspective.

Lewis also compared the joy he found in reading with what he experienced in worship or love: "I transcend myself [when I read] and am never more myself than when I do."[1] Maybe you too have begun to see how, in some mysterious way, God can use great music, books, and even film to get us out of ourselves so he can mold and shape us into the people he intends for us to be.

Sadly, not everyone shares this joy of music. I talk with some of my friends who treat Christian music as little more than elevator or background music. So, a song that floors me with its emotional power and underlying message leaves my friend listening to the same tune completely unfazed. This difference in perspective reminds me of something C. S. Lewis once said of a nonreader: "He may be full of goodness and good sense, but he inhabits a tiny world. In it, we should be suffocated."[2]

In the end, my overriding hope for this book is that *The Gospel Unplugged* helps you avoid "suffocating in a tiny world"—that you can now experience the transforming power of Christian music in a way that you never did before. As you listen to your favorite songs, invite God to use them as tools for shaping and molding you in your faith. In other words, turn up the volume on the songs that rock your soul.

Notes

Introduction

1. C. S. Lewis, *An Experiment in Criticism* (Cambridge: Cambridge University Press, 1961), 2.

2. "Time Out for Mozart," *The Shawshank Redemption*, DVD, directed by Frank Darabont, 1994.

Chapter 1: Clocking God

1. David McCasland, *Oswald Chambers: Abandoned to God* (Grand Rapids: Discovery House Publishers, 1993), 273.

Chapter 3: Mind the Gap

1. Rainer Maria Rilke, *Rilke and Benvenuta: An Intimate Correspondence* (New York: Fromm International, 1987).

Chapter 4: Get Busy Living

1. "What They Take," *The Shawshank Redemption*.

2. "Exactly What They Take," *Shawshank Redemption*.

3. "The Danger of Hope," *Shawshank Redemption*.

4. Charles Colson with Ellen Santilli Vaughn, *The Body* (Dallas: Word, 1992), 203ff.

5. "The Danger of Hope," *Shawshank Redemption*.

6. C. S. Lewis, *The Screwtape Letters* (San Francisco: HarperSanFrancisco, 2001), 61.

7. Frank "Buzz" Trexler, "The Buzz Trexler Experience," members.aol.com/ripshin/scc97.htm.

8. "A Free Man's Dreams," *Shawshank Redemption*.

Chapter 6: A Rembrandt in Disguise

1. C. S. Lewis, *The Voyage of the Dawn Treader* (New York: Collier Books, 1952), 90.

2. Ibid., 91.

Chapter 7: (More Than) Creatures for a While

1. Winfried Corduan, *No Doubt About It* (Nashville: Broadman and Holman, 1997), 21.

Chapter 8: True Greatness

1. Oswald Chambers, *Our Brilliant Heritage* (Fort Washington, PA: Christian Literature Crusade, 1929), 82.

2. Fyodor Dostoevsky, quoted in Philip Yancey's *What's So Amazing about Grace?* (Grand Rapids: Zondervan, 1997), 175.

3. C. S. Lewis, *Mere Christianity* (Nashville: Broadman and Holman, 1996), 116.

Chapter 9: More

1. *Braveheart*, VHS, directed by Mel Gibson, 1995.

Chapter 10: Future Glory

1. McCasland, *Oswald Chambers*, 168.

2. Elisabeth Elliot, *Through Gates of Splendor* (Wheaton: Tyndale, 1981), 20.

Chapter 12: Nagging Doubts

1. Philip Yancey, *Reaching for an Invisible God* (Grand Rapids: Zondervan, 2000), 54.

2. Ibid, 41.

3. C. S. Lewis, *The Letters of C. S. Lewis to Arthur Greeves* (New York: Collier/Macmillan, 1986), 398–99.

4. Ibid.

5. T. S. Elliot, *Four Quartets* (Orlando: Harcourt, 1971), 32.

Chapter 14: Spread-Eagled Disciples

1. Oswald Chambers, *My Utmost for His Highest* (Uhrichsville, OH: Barbour, 1992), 202.

Chapter 15: Thrill Seekers

1. C. S. Lewis, *Christian Reflections* (Grand Rapids: Eerdmans, 1967), 42–43.
2. McCasland, *Oswald Chambers*, 195.
3. John Eldredge, *Wild at Heart* (Nashville: Thomas Nelson, 2001), 200.

Chapter 16: The Icarus Confession

1. Oswald Chambers, *The Place of Help* (Fort Washington, PA: Christian Literature Crusade, 1929), 132.
2. Dietrich Bonhoeffer, *The Cost of Discipleship* (New York: Macmillan, 1963), 99.
3. Lewis, *Screwtape Letters*, 65.

Chapter 17: Out of Your Comfort Zone

1. Philip Yancey, *What's So Amazing about Grace?* (Grand Rapids: Zondervan, 1997), 175.
2. Victor Hugo, *Les Misérables* (New York: Barnes and Noble Books, 1996), 90.
3. Ibid, 69.

Chapter 18: A Modern Pharisee

1. Nichole Nordeman, from the liner notes of *Wide Eyed*.

Chapter 19: A Noisy Walk

1. Lewis, *Screwtape Letters*, 119–20.

Chapter 20: The Simple Life

1. McCasland, *Oswald Chambers*, 206.

Afterword

1. Lewis, *Experiment in Criticism*, 3.
2. Ibid.

Permissions

Songs are listed in order of appearance:

1. "Naïve" by Chris Rice
© 1998 Clumsy Fly Music (Admin. By Word Music, LLC)
All Rights Reserved. Used by Permission.

2. "Gomer's Theme"
Written by: Samuel Anderson/ Johnny Powell/ Mark Lee/ Bradley Avery/ David Carr
© Gray Dot Songs (ASCAP)/ Vandura 2500 Songs (ASCAP)/ New Spring, a division
of Zomba Enterprises, Inc. (ASCAP)

3. "Hymn"
Written by: Charlie Lowell/ Dan Haseltine/ Matt Odmark/ Stephen Mason
© Pogostick Music (BMI)/ Bridge Building, a division of Zomba Enterprises, Inc.
(BMI)

4. "Free"
Written by: Steven Curtis Chapman
© 1996 Sparrow Song (BMI)/ Peach Hill Songs (BMI)
(Admin. by EMI)

5. "40 Acres" by Aaron Tate
© 1999 Cumbee Road Music (admin. by Music Services)
All Rights Reserved. Used By Permission.

6. "Anyway"
Written by: Nichole Nordeman
© 1998 Ariose Music (ASCAP)
(Admin. by EMI)

7. "Original Species"
Written by: Will McGinniss/ Mark Stuart/ Bob Herdman
© 1997 Up in the Mix Music (BMI)/ Flicker USA Publishing (BMI)

8. "Great" by Lamont Heibert
© 2000 Integrity's Hosanna! Music/ASCAP

9. "Meant to Live"
Written by: Jonathan Foreman/ Tim Foreman
© 2003 Meadowgreen Music Company (ASCAP)/ Sugar Pete Songs (ASCAP)
(Admin. by EMI)

10. "We Have Forgotten" by Matt Slocum
© 1998 My So-Called Music (Admin. By Squint Songs), Squint Music
All Rights Reserved. Used by Permission.

11. "Legacy"
Written by: Nichole Nordeman
© 2002 Ariose Music (ASCAP)
(Admin. by EMI)

12. "Hallelujah"
Written by: Peter Furler/ Phil (Joel) Urry/ Jeff Frankenstein
© 1998 Dawn Treader Music (SESAC)/ Shepherd's Fold Music (BMI)/ Campbell Music
(BMI)/ Oinch Music

13. "Smell the Color Nine" by Chris Rice
© 2000 Clumsy Fly Music (Admin. By Word Music, LLC)
All Rights Reserved. Used by Permission.

14. "Big Enough" by Chris Rice
© 1998 Clumsy Fly Music (Admin. By Word Music, LLC)
All Rights Reserved. Used by Permission.

15. "Prove Me Wrong" by Aaron Tate
© 2000 Cumbee Road Music (admin. by Music Services)
All Rights Reserved. Used By Permission.

16. "Coming Home" by Aaron Tate
© 1996 Cumbee Road Music (admin. by Music Services)
All Rights Reserved. Used By Permission.

17. "Frail"
Written by: Charlie Lowell/ Dan Haseltine/ Matt Odmark/ Stephen Mason
© Pogostick Music (BMI)/ Bridge Building, a division of Zomba Enterprises, Inc.
(BMI)

18. "Dive"
Written by: Steven Curtis Chapman
© 1999 Sparrow Song (BMI)/ Peach Hill Songs (BMI)
(Admin. by EMI)

19. "Deep End"
Written by: Peter Furler/ Phil (Joel) Urry/ Jody Davis/ Jeff Frankenstein
© 1998 Dawn Treader Music (SESAC)/ Shepherd's Fold Music (BMI)/ Campbell Music
(BMI)/ Helmet Publishing (BMI)

20. "Worlds Apart"
Written by: Charlie Lowell/ Dan Haseltine/ Matt Odmark/ Stephen Mason
© Pogostick Music (BMI)/ Bridge Building, a division of Zomba Enterprises, Inc.
(BMI)

21. "Saving Grace"
Written by Matt Huesmann and Grant Cunningham
© 1998 Matt Huesmann Music (ASCAP)/Administered by EMI & BUG
All Rights Reserved. Used by Permission.

22. "Wide Eyed"
Written by: Nichole Nordeman
© 1998 Ariose Music (ASCAP)
(Admin. by EMI)

23. "Adding to the Noise"
Written by: Jonathan Foreman/ Tim Foreman
© 2003 Meadowgreen Music Company (ASCAP)/ Sugar Pete Songs (ASCAP)
(Admin. by EMI)

24. "Chevette"
Written by: Will McGinniss/ Mark Stuart/ Bob Herdman/ Brian McSweeney
© 1997 Up in the Mix Music (BMI)/ Flicker USA Publishing (BMI)/ Starstruck Music
(ASCAP)

Rich Wagner is author of many books, including *Christianity for Dummies*, that are designed to make meaty Christian truth easily digestible for postmodern readers. His online home is at digitalwalk.com, a discipleship-oriented website for challenging and encouraging Christians living in this digital age. Rich lives in Princeton, Massachusetts.

www.gospelunplugged.com